C000199892

Peter J. Foss

THE FIELD OF REDEMORE:
The Battle of Bosworth, 1485

second edition

Foreword by Professor Ralph A. Griffiths

Kairos Press
Newtown Linford
Leicestershire
1998

Copyright© P. J. Foss, 1990

Second edition, 1998
ISBN 1-871344-06-9

(Originally published in 1990 by Rosalba Press, the publishing group
of the Yorkshire Branch of the Richard III society)

To Michael and Nicola

Front Cover: detail from a mural of the battle of Bosworth, by an
unknown early twentieth century artist. The painting is in the Three
Tuns Inn, Long Street, Atherstone, traditionally thought to be Henry
Tudor's lodgings on the night before the battle. Reproduced by kind
permission of the proprietors.

Design and Layout by Robin Stevenson, Kairos Press.
Body Text in Aldine 721 BT, 10.5pt.
Imagingsetting by CDS Imaging, Leicester.
Printed in Great Britain by Norwood Press, Anstey, Leicester.

British Library Cataloguing in Publication Data
A CIP catalogue record for this book is available from the British Library

The right of Peter J. Foss to be identified as the author of this work has been asserted by
him in accordance with the Copyright, Designs and Patents Act, 1988. The reproduction
of any material contained in this book, by any means, is forbidden without permission in
writing from the copyright holder.

Kairos Press
552 Bradgate Road
Newtown Linford
Leicestershire LE6 0HB
Great Britain

CONTENTS

ILLUSTRATIONS

MAPS

4

Foreword

by Professor Ralph A. Griffiths
University of Wales, Swansea

Richard III is unlikely ever to lose his grip on people's historical imagination. His character and brief reign make for compelling drama. It was so in his own lifetime and the fascination is no less five hundred years on – indeed, in theatre, on screen and in print, the Richard III industry is at full throttle. Part of the fascination lies in the unresolved – and probably unresolvable – questions that can be asked about the man, his deeds and his attitudes. Yet, the task of probing the realities of Richard's life and reign is, and always has been, an urgent one, for Ricardian myths abound, prejudice sometimes passes for history, and scholarly reserve can be decidedly unhelpful.

Medieval biography is an elusive art. In the case of Richard III, so many decisions were taken privately and without written record that it is doubtful that much is to be gained from re-working the little that is known about the king at the most critical points in his life. Far greater opportunity lies in the circumstances of his reign and of the previous decade when he was Edward IV's staunchest lieutenant. One of the most dramatic and decisive events in Richard's life was that field in Leicestershire, not far south of Market Bosworth, where he spent his last hours. It is to the credit of the Yorkshire branch of the Richard III Society that it sponsored the original publication of Peter Foss's authoritative study of the battle.

Bosworth ranks with Hastings, Waterloo and El Alamein as one of the decisive battles of British history: the death of one king and the accession of another; the ending of one dynasty and the beginning of another; and a heralding of the end of the Wars of the Roses. The battle has even been invested with broader constitutional, cultural and social significance, not always with good reason. Yet our knowledge of what happened on 22 August 1485 is fragmentary, even confused: the most detailed report that survives was penned by an Italian visiting England some twenty years later.

Some might say that the quest to uncover the details and precise location of the action that day is of no great consequence: the outcome is the thing. This is not so. Prejudice and fancy feed on vagueness, and reputations can be built on error, and if history's contribution to tourism and leisure is flawed, then popular perceptions of the past will be warped. It is the merit of Peter Foss's book that it places the study of the Battle of Bosworth on surer historical foundations, by adopting a variety of approaches and marshalling an impressive range of evidence and from the vantage point, too, of a Leicestershire man.

The surge of interest in Richard and Bosworth during 1985 drew attention to the uncertain basis for the common assumption – lavishly represented by Leicestershire County Council's Battlefield Centre – that the encounter between Richard III and Henry Tudor took place on Ambion Hill. Peter Foss re-examines the evidence and proposes a new scenario for the armies' movements before the battle, the battle itself, and the dispersal of the combatants across the 'field of Redemore' until some found a final resting place in Dadlington churchyard, whilst Henry Tudor marched triumphantly to Leicester, with Richard's body slung across a horse's back. He uses the testimony of antiquaries (whom modern historians too often ignore at their peril), picks his way through local tradition, pursues myths and legends to their source and, most impressive of all, combines the testimony of contemporary writers with his own skilful reconstruction of the landscape of this corner of Leicestershire as it was in the fifteenth century. The result is an object lesson in interdisciplinary study which makes a lasting contribution to our history.

Preface to the Second Edition

Since the publication of the first edition of *The Field of Redemore* in 1990 there has been a growing body of opinion that the account of the battle of Bosworth given in this book provides a more convincing interpretation of the evidence than has so far been the case. In addition, the nature of that evidence, some of it new, some of it reconsidered, has been recognised to have implications for the way historic battlefields are managed and publicised which go beyond the niceties of academic debate.

This was well illustrated by the publication in 1994 of English Heritage's proposals for a Historic Battlefields Register, where Bosworth was described as 'second only in importance to Hastings' in English history. On the map published with the Register, the boundary of the battlefield area of Bosworth embraced for the first time the 'Redemore' in the Leicestershire parishes of Stoke Golding, Dadlington, and Shenton, and proposed a long-distance trail, following for much of its way a route that the author had established as a 'Redemore trail' in 1985.

Furthermore, the interpretative overlay in the Register leaflet drew attention to the importance of the Site of Special Scientific Interest at Kendall's Meadow, the field names associated with the indigenous marshland, and the location of the battlefield chantry of c.1511 at Dadlington church, all significant in the interpretation given in Chapters 3 and 4 of the present book. English Heritage's report recognised the difficulties that exist about interpreting the evidence for the position of the armies and manoeuvres at the battle of Bosworth but clearly favoured the scenario put forward here, as for example the position of the encounter between Norfolk and Oxford in the battle vanguard, based upon an idea first suggested by Professor Goodman (see Chapter 4). The importance of this endorsement by English Heritage, the chief state agency for the protection of places of historic interest, is of immense significance, particularly in the light of 'material consideration status' recently awarded by government (1995) to the land within the designated battlefield boundaries, ensuring for Bosworth the protection of an area now covering half of Dadlington old parish and much of Shenton, as well as Ambion Hill.

The interest that links the public imagination with historic battlefields was shown not only by the media response to the Battlefields Register but by the controversy over Bosworth that has continued since 1985. The launch of the Register in September 1994 was accompanied by headline articles in national newspapers focussing almost exclusively on Bosworth ('How History Lost Site of Richard III's Last Stand', *Sunday Telegraph*, 4 Sept 1994; 'Plantagenets Ready for Fight as New Register Puts Bosworth Killing Field Half a Mile Away', *Guardian*, 5 Sept 1994).

The publication of a second edition of *The Field of Redemore* gives me the opportunity to make some minor additions and corrections. Apart from these adjustments, the text is unchanged; and it remains for me only to thank a number of people whose help has been gratefully received since 1990: Mr & Mrs E.G. Parry; Mr & Mrs W.G. Webster; Mr T.C. Hickman; Mr Robin Stevenson; and Mr A.D. White.

P. J. Foss
Gloucester, 1997

Preface to the First Edition

The present book is a response to a problem. The particular question is that posed in recent years concerning the site of the battle of Bosworth; and the general problem involves the nature of historical evidence and how that evidence is to be assessed.

In 1985 I produced a pamphlet in time for the quincentenary celebrations of the battle of Bosworth, in which I suggested an alternative site for the battle; consequently I was involved in a small way in the controversy that arose around this subject. With others, I was dissatisfied with some of the accepted readings of the evidence, and in particular with the failure of some public bodies to meet the challenge of new thinking on the subject. In recent years there has occurred a number of significant advances in our understanding of the evidence for the battle of Bosworth, and stimulating ideas have been aired in books and articles by Colin Richmond, Michael Bennett, Ralph Griffiths and Oliver Harris, and also in the pages of *The Ricardian.*

The following study is my own assessment of this material, together with a suggestion as to how the historical topography of the area can be employed in the corpus of evidence. Several articles which formed the basis of the book first appeared in the Market Bosworth and District Magazine, *Aspect* (November 1985-July 1986), and a study of the Sutton Cheney Estates has been another fruit of the enterprise.

A work of this kind involves the help and advice of many institutions and individuals – both academic and lay, national and local – and I would like here to acknowledge them, with thanks, in alphabetical order: Mr Michael Archer of the Victoria and Albert Museum, Dr Lorraine Attreed, Mr John Audsley, Mrs Jill Bourne, Ms Ruth M. Brown of the Royal Armouries, Mr R. Burgess, Revd. Anthony Bardsley, Mr Barry Burkhill, Dr Steve Bartle of Leeds University, Mr Paul T. Bale, the Librarians of the Bodleian Library, Mr D. Chaplin, Mrs E. Chaplin, Mr A.M. Cockerill, Ms Margaret Condon of the Public Record Office, Mr A.F. Cook, Dr Christopher Dyer of Birmingham University, Capt. C.B. Fetherston-Dilke, Mrs R.J. Freedman of York City Archives, Ms Margaret Gelling, Mr J. Gladman, Mr Ray Gosling, Professor R.A. Griffiths of University College, Swansea, Mr Fred Hartley of Leicestershire Museums, Mr T.R.J. Hall, Mr Trevor Hill, Mrs Philippa Hodgetts, Mr W.H. Kelliher of the British Library, Mr Richard Knowles, Mr Peter Liddle of the Jewry Wall Museum, Mr Phillip Lindley, Mr W. Long, Mrs Kathryn Murton of the British Library, Dr Robin Old of the British Geological Survey, Ms Mary O'Regan, Mrs Jean Parry, Mr Thom. Richardson of the Royal Armouries, Mr R.A. Rutland of Leicestershire Museums, Dr Colin Richmond of Keele University, Mr R.G. Rutter, Mr A.E. Squires, the Archivists of Staffordshire Record Office, Dr Diane Thurston, Mr J. Tallis of Manchester University, Miss Kate Thompson of Leicestershire Record Office, Mr and Mrs Gordon Webster, Miss Sarah Webster, Mr Stanley Woodward, Mr Frederick Wollaston, Mr and Mrs J.V. Wright, Mr K.S. Wright, Capt. F.O.S. Wynne, and Mr. R.C. Yorke of the College of Arms.

I am especially grateful for the help of Tim Parry throughout all stages of the research, and also for the support of the secretary and trustees of the Richard III and Yorkist History Trust, who awarded me a grant in 1987 to pursue research on the Hinckley-Lyre Agreement.

Peter J. Foss
Lampeter, 1990

Plate 1. Where the battle slain were buried: Dadlington Church.
An engraving of 1791, from John Nichols, *The History and Antiquities of the County of Leicester* IV (1811)

CHAPTER ONE

Chroniclers and Poets:
The Problem of the Sources

It is an axiom that history is a palimpsest of data and opinion. The casual details that have come down to us from the past have been filtered through so many attempted realisations that one may well wonder what kind of construct it is that history presents to us. An event as distant and as historically decisive as the battle of Bosworth has its own problems of myth and legend; in addition to which a just assessment of the relevant data may be hopelessly distorted if the data were proved to be sufficiently unbalanced and fragmentary. Of course, we are not usually in a position to know. However, there are ways and means of assessing what we have and distinguishing between authoritative material, and the glosses, fiction and fantasy which often comprise a fair body of the myth. When such a myth offends common sense, or is independent of more verifiable material, it has to be treated with suspicion, and frequently in the final analysis rendered inadmissible.

Still, myths are potent because they often contain the seeds of truth. A function of historical scrutiny is to find out if that truth exists, and what it is. Sometimes the myth goes back a long way, and it is part of ubiquitous 'tradition', but in fact can be found to arise out of a gloss of the earliest sources, which in themselves may present problems of admissibility. I want to show here how adaptations of the earliest evidence for the battle of Bosworth – adaptations made by sixteenth century chroniclers – tended to distort and confuse the later picture of the battle. But I also want to show how myths that became embedded in public consciousness (though ignored by the chroniclers) may coincide with other independent evidence and may be measured against the criteria of common sense. For this purpose I begin with Shakespeare, because it is Shakespeare's portrayal of the Wars of the Roses which reflected the Tudor historiographical tradition, and which consolidated it for later generations.

Shakespeare's treatment of the battle of Bosworth in his *Life and Death of Richard the Thirde* is interesting for what divergences or coincidences may be detected in relation to independent data about the battle. Shakespeare read the available chronicles of his day – Grafton, Holinshed, and perhaps More's *Historie of King Richard the Third*[1] – and used the dramatically appropriate details of the traditional account to support his portrait of a Machiavellian usurper. But Shakespeare also reflected a common body of knowledge in the late sixteenth century; and his picture of the battle is potentially as trusted a source for what was thought to have happened as any other record of the Elizabethan period.

Shakespeare's drama capitalised on the powerful and personalised aspects of the story such as Richard's nightmare on the eve of the battle and the orations to the armies. In some details, however, he mirrored a common knowledge which, in the light of other data, rings true. He was aware of Christopher Urswick's go-between role in the days leading up to the battle;[2] he puts Lord Stanley's forces 'half a mile south' of those of the king;[3] and he refers twice to the loss of the king's horse.[4]

Of the two aspects which had prime dramatic potential, the orations of the respective commanders before the battle represent a gloss on the original source. They are given at length in Holinshed (1577), though copied almost word-for-word from Edward Hall's account in *The Union of the Two Noble and Illustre Families of Lancastre and York* of 1548.[5] However, Hall seems to be their inventor, since *his* source, Polydore Vergil's *Anglica Historia* of 1534, makes no mention of such speeches.[6] It may be that such orations were customary but we have no way of knowing what either Henry Tudor or Richard III said to their men before battle commenced, and it is therefore misleading to infer notions about, for example, the disposition of armies, and the frame of mind of the commanders, from Hall's insertion into Vergil's narrative.[7]

On the other hand, the tradition of Richard III's nightmare on the eve of the battle is supported by several independent early sources, as well as by Polydore Vergil. It is first recorded in the *Crowland Chronicle* (second continuation, 1486) where, however, it is reported at second hand *(ut asseritur)*.[8] It is said that during the night the king had experienced *terrenda somnia*, terrible dreams – with a multitude of demons surrounding him. In the morning, he 'presented a countenance, which, always drawn, was then even more livid and ghastly'.[9] Although the story was probably legendary by the time Polydore Vergil was using *viva voce* information at court in c.1503, the fact that he reports it does suggest there was good foundation for the story (otherwise he might have referred to it as 'vulgar fame').[10] Vergil was critical of myths and chose to see Richard's dream as the workings of a guilty conscience rather than as a display of portents.

Linked with this story is the reported confusion of the morning after, since the *Crowland Chronicle* also records that Richard had neither breakfast nor the celebration of Mass prepared for him that morning.[11] The *Crowland Chronicle* is a good authority for such details because of its near-contemporary composition and the substance of its background knowledge of events at court under Edward IV and Richard III.[12] The story is given further credence, however, by a remarkable reminiscence preserved in a manuscript book in the British Library entitled *Lord Morley on Transubstantiation*.[13] This was written for Queen Mary c.1553 and is a compilation of *exempla* which illustrate the power of the Mass and the operation of divine justice. The example of Richard's disastrous breakfast must therefore be read in this context, but it does purport to record a memoir by one Bygott, who had been in the service of Queen Anne and then of Richard III at the battle:

> Bigott sayd that kyng Richard callyd in the mornyng for to have had masse sayd before hym, but when his chapelyne had one thing ready, evermore & they wanted another, when they had wyne they lacked breade, And ever one thing was myssing.

There are other episodes in Shakespeare's description which add drama to the action and which are derived from the chronicles, but which have less authority. For example, the distich attached to Norfolk's tent ('Jack of Norffolke, be not to bolde/ for Dyken thy mayster is bought and solde') is again an invention of Hall's;[14] and the idea of a personal combat between the chief protagonists, which would be mandatory in a dramatic presentation, is probably unlikely given the circumstantial evidence of the battle. In fact, Hall's adaptation of this episode from Polydore Vergil is a subtle misrepresentation of his text. Hall's *Chronicle* recounts that in the course of King Richard's assault on Henry's position, Henry 'kept him at the swerdes poinct without avantage'; whereas Vergil's phrase reads drily, 'Henry sustained the attack longer than even his soldiers would have thought'.[15] Similarly, Hall's words are that Henry offered contest 'body to body and man to man', whereas Vergil's account is simply that he 'keenly offered himself to the struggle, since all hope of safety lay in arms', which of course could be said to imply that Henry had no other course of action in the circumstances.[16] It is obvious then that Vergil's brief but precise words have been corrupted to give a picture of a personal combat that might never have happened. It was the task of a body-guard (Vergil's phrase *stipatum armatus*) to protect the person of the king from such an attack.[17]

This question of the translation and adaptation of Polydore Vergil's account will recur again in the course of our study. It is a crucial one since several of the sixteenth century myths about the battle of Bosworth originate in these subtle corruptions of a primary source. The addition of orations in Hall is an obvious case in point, but embroideries such as that concerning the direction of the sun in relation to Henry Tudor's advance – where Hall adds the phrase 'and in the faces of his enemies' to Vergil's line about Henry putting the marsh on his right-hand side and thereby the sun at his back *(solem a tergo reliquit)* – may give an impression not intended in the original.[18] Furthermore, Vergil's description of the king's precipitate move against Henry Tudor at the height of the battle *(ex altero latere...incurrit)* was awkwardly rendered by the anonymous sixteenth century translator of Vergil, and was neutralised by

Hall. The phrase is in fact crucial for an understanding of the course of the battle at this point, and can only be translated as 'he charged out of the other side'. The Tudor translator, however, gives 'owt of thone syde withowt the vanwardes', whilst Hall writes merely 'out of ye syde'.[19] Neither conveys the meaning of the Latin correctly.

A late sixteenth century dramatisation of the events of the battle of Bosworth, such as that contained in Shakespeare's play, in drawing on the chronicle tradition, endorsed such corruptions and elaborations as it contained, and compounded them into the myth that came to be handed down. But Shakespeare also drew on a widely-accepted oral tradition which finds expression partly in the Stanley ballads[20] and which perpetuated details omitted from the well-known chronicles. For example, that the battle took place on a 'plain' is, technically speaking, not given in any of the primary sources, but was accepted by Shakespeare and other Elizabethan writers. The poet Michael Drayton who was born in 1563 at Hartshill, not far from the scene of the battle, describes the armies being drawn up 'on a spacious Moore, lying Southward from the towne' (i.e.Bosworth);[21] and Sir George Buck in his *History of King Richard Third* (1619) describes the king's death as actually taking place 'upon the plain'.[22] Authoritative independent evidence such as that of William Burton confirms this tradition, when he writes in *The Description of Leicestershire* (1622) that the battle was fought 'in a large, flat, plaine, and spacious ground, three miles distant from [Bosworth]'.[23] Admittedly, these are late testimonies, although some of them are locally based and therefore to that extent authoritative, but the belief does seem to reflect a tradition current in the 1540s when Hall first mentioned a 'plain' in his account.[24] It would be tempting to regard such an interpolation as spurious were it not for these later writers, and the evidence of the ballads, to which I will return in Chapter Three. The same judgement, I have suggested, could be accorded to other details in Shakespeare, where independent evidence unknown to him seems to confirm aspects of a tradition he is reflecting.

The sixteenth century chroniclers have to be put into perspective within the context of their Tudor provenance and Tudor bias. In addition to copying Polydore Vergil, most of them also drew on a body of opinion which originated at the political centre of affairs in London, and was incorporated to some extent in the series of London chronicles which survive from the early part of the sixteenth century.[25] The earliest of these was the so-called *Great Chronicle* with its account of the battle of Bosworth dating from before 1496.[26] However, as Kingsford pointed out, the *Great Chronicle* and its successors were less authoritative about events at a distance than those which took place in or near London and so fell more or less within the writer's own knowledge.[27] Thus, significantly, the *Great Chronicle* devoted several lines to

OF FABYANS CRONICLE CCXXVII.

pzynce and hys company, whanne he
was commyn vnto the lande/he incō
tynently kneled downe vpon þ erth/
& wyth meke countenaunce & pure de
uocyon began thys pſalme : Iudica me
deus, & decerne causam meam. &c. ¶The
whyche whan he had fynyſſhed to þ
ende, and kyſſed the grounde mekely,
and reuerently made the ſigne of the
croſſe vpon hym/ he commaunded
ſuche as were aboute hym, boldly in
the name of god & ſaynte George to
ſet forewarde.

whan the landyng of thys pzynce
was blowen about the lande / many
was the man that drewe vnto hym,
aſwell ſuche as were in ſondzy ſeyn-
twaryes as other that were abzode/
ſo that hys ſtrēgth encreaſed ſhortly.
¶Than the kyng gadered hys power
in all haſte/ and ſpedde hym in ſuche
wyſe, that vpon the.xxii. daye of Au-
guſt & begynnyng of the thyzde yere
of hys reygne/he mette wyth the ſaid
pzynce nere vnto a vyllage in Leyce
terſhyre named Boſwozth, nere vnto
Leyceter. where betwene theym was
foughten a ſharpe batayll/ & ſharper
ſhulde haue ben, yf the kynges partie
had ben faſt to hym. But many towarde the felde refuſyd hym, & yode
vnto that other partye. And ſome
ſtode houpynge a ferre of, tyl they ſaw
to the whyche partye the vyctozy
fyll.

In concluſyon kynge Rycharde
was ſlayne/and vppon hys partye þ
duke of Nozthfolke befoze tyme named lozde Hawarde, wyth Bzakyng
bury Lieutenaunt of the towre, and
many other. And amonge other was
there taken on lyue the erle of Sur-
rey ſonne to the forefayde duke of
Nozthfolke, & ſent vnto the towze of
London/where he remayned as pzy
ſoner longe tyme after.

Than was the corps of Rycharde
late kyng ſpoyled, & naked as he was
bozne caſte behynde a man / and ſo
caryed vnreuerently ouertwharte þ
hozſe backe vnto the fryers at Leyce
ter. where after a ſeaſon that he had
lyen that all men myght beholde him
he was there wyth lytell reuerence
buryed. And thus wyth miſery ended
thys pzynce/ whych ruled moſt what
by rygour aud tyzannye, whan he in
great trouble & agony had reygned
oz vſurped by the ſpace of.ii.yeres.ii.
monethes and.ii.dayes.

And than was the noble pzynce
Henry admytted for kynge, and ſo
pzoclaymed kyng by the name of Hē
ry the.vii. ¶The whych ſped hi ſhoztly
to London/ſo that vppon the.xxviii.
daye of the ſayd moneth of Auguſte,
he was by the mayre and the citeſyns
met in good araye/as the mayre and
aldermen in ſcarlet, and the cyteſyns
in vyolet, at harneſey parke/& frome
thens conueyed thozugh the cytye
vnto the byſſhop of Londōs palays,
and there for that tyme lodged.

And vpon the.xi. day of Octobze
nert folowyng, than beyng the ſwe-
tynge ſykeneſſe of newe begon / dyed
the ſayd Thomas Hylle than of Lon
don mayre. And for hym was choſen
as mayre ſyz wyllyam Stokker
knyght & Dzaper, whyche dyed alſo
of the ſayd ſykeneſſe ſhortly after.
And than John warde Grocer was
choſen mayre / whyche ſo contynued
tyll the feeſt of Symonde and Jude
folowynge.

Francia.
⟜Charles the.ix.

Arolus oz Char-
les þ.ix.oz.viii. of
þ name, ſonſi vnto
the.xi.Lowys/be-
gā his reygn ouer
þ realm of Fraūce
the fourth daye of
Septēbze

Plate 2. The Chronicle of Robert Fabyan, 1516, which popularised the standard Tudor version of the events of 1485. Shown here is a page from the second edition (1533) in the National Library of Scotland, where a 16th century hand has written a marginal note on Bosworth:
'the battay[le] of Redesmore heath was bytwene K.R. & K.H. th[e] vijth'
Courtesy of the Trustees of the National Library of Scotland

the desertions from Brackenbury's camp before the battle, since Brackenbury, in his capacity as lord lieutenant of the Tower, would have been a recognisable figure to Londoners in the 1490s.[28] The *Great Chronicle's* emphasis is therefore on the *relevance* of the information which reached London shortly after the event. This is reflected in its description of the tardiness of Richard's support (and therefore his unpopularity) and on the piety of the new king (and therefore his suitability to assume the throne).

The most notable of the London-based chronicles which made use of the *Great Chronicle* material was that of Robert Fabyan, which by his own account was completed in 1504.[29] Fabyan compiled a rough and ready narrative from reports available in London at the time, and this was published in 1516 by the royal printer Robert Pynson. Fabyan was popular and was reprinted numerous times in the following years; and it was through his version that the London chronicles material was widely disseminated in the sixteenth century. However, if we compare Fabyan with the *Great Chronicle* account we recognise that whilst some information is abbreviated or omitted, two aspects are considerably expanded: Henry's piety on his landing at Milford Haven, when he 'kyssed the grounde mekely and reverently made the Signe of the Crosse upon hym', and the extent of the lack of support Richard suffered ('but many towarde the felde refusyd hym and yode unto that other partie/ And some stode hovynge a feere of/ tyll they sawe to whiche partye the victory fyll').[30] Thus the contrast between the popularity of the two kings was emphasised by Fabyan, whilst details relating to the actions of the participants and the progress of the battle (some available to the *Great Chronicle* author) were omitted.

Polydore Vergil also made use of the London-based material when he came to write about contemporary events in the *Anglica Historia*, published after long delay in the Basle edition of 1534.[31] Vergil started gathering information shortly after his arrival in England in 1502. It is thought, therefore, that the first draft of his chapter on Richard III was composed c.1508-10.[32] The originality of Vergil's book in comparison with contemporary records is that it was essentially a *history* rather than a chronicle; that is, it was the first narrative of its kind which discriminated between different kinds of data on the basis of truth or according to the criteria of probability, and it arranged that data in a methodical form. Consequently the formlessness of earlier chronicles is thrown into sharp relief; Fabyan's rehearsing of the old stories of Britain's legendary past seems archaic next to Vergil's Renaissance scepticism.[33]

Although Polydore Vergil was writing under Tudor patronage and clearly supported Henry VII's succession, his portrait of the young king in the early days of his reign is candid rather than flattering. In fact there is some evidence that Vergil was allowed more leeway for criticism than would have been the case with an English-speaking historian at court.[34] As regards the battle of Bosworth there is no reason why Vergil should fabricate the data at his disposal. Indeed, writing according to historiographical precepts laid down by Cicero, he was duty-bound to be scrupulously fair to his material, particularly when writing about battles.[35] In some respects, Vergil's account was less favourable to Henry Tudor than were the London chronicles before him. For example he relates the story of Henry's near-desertion of his army at Tamworth, and suggests that Henry, though brave, was essentially a man of fortune who owed his power to the treachery of Richard's friends as much as to the will of God.[36]

Polydore Vergil's description of the battle of Bosworth is the most detailed of the early accounts and, because of its clarity and relative impartiality, represents an important primary source. I shall use Vergil's description as the basis for the interpretation I provide. Everything about it, whether we agree with it or not, is coherent. It begins on the eve of the battle with the king's nightmares in camp, from which Vergil draws the moral that evil deeds produce a disturbed conscience in the evil doer.

There follows a detailed depiction of the king's array of battle, with the explanation that Richard's long battle-line was intended to cast fear into the hearts of the onlookers. Lord Thomas Stanley's refusal to commit himself openly is described, and the effect this had on Henry's morale. Stanley is said to have taken up a position *ut medius loco*, midway between the two armies; after which there is a description of Henry's formation, and the relative size of his and Stanley's forces in comparison with the king's superior numbers. The only topographical feature mentioned by Vergil at the site of the battle is the marsh – *palus* – and this is described precisely because it had strategic importance. It acted as a defence to Henry's forces at the point where they changed direction, and in so doing they put the sun at their back.

After the start of the battle, Vergil allows himself some account of the Earl of Oxford's tactics, which he recognises were somewhat decisive in the course of events. There follows a description of Richard's precipitate move 'beyond the battle-line'[37] against Henry's position, and the *melée* that followed. The intervention of Sir William Stanley's army brings the battle to its crisis, and the king, desperately but courageously, is killed 'fighting amongst the most densely-packed of the enemy'.[38] Meanwhile, the victory of the vanguard under Oxford occasions a rout, though no direction is specified, and the day ends with Henry's withdrawal to a nearby hill *(in proximum collem)* where he gives thanks to God and is promptly crowned. Near the end of the narrative, Vergil describes separately the report *(fama)* that Richard could have saved himself and that a swift horse was brought to him for this purpose, but that he refused to do so and instead 'descended' into the battle in order to make an end either 'of war or life'.[39]

As we shall see, Polydore Vergil's language was both meticulous and precise, but those chroniclers that borrowed from him were employing a vernacular vocabulary which in the sixteenth century had a continually shifting semantic base.[40] Furthermore, their renderings of his text were governed less by critical precision than by attempts to narrate a stirring story effectively, and, in the wake of Hall, of glorifying the Tudor succession. The mid-sixteenth century anonymous translation of Polydore Vergil, which has been so influential in its transmission of Vergil's text, is awkward by comparison and seriously affects the clarity of Vergil's meaning in some crucial areas. This translation may very well have been known to John Stow and other Elizabethan antiquaries, but was not in fact published until 1844.[41] Stow's *Annales* of 1592, in its circumspect use of Vergil's account, may have been influenced by the growing denigration of the *Anglica Historia* towards the end of the sixteenth century; and one can detect instead a marked reliance on the London perspective of events, and on Fabyan's *Chronicle* in particular.[42]

However, another popular chronicle of the time, John Speed's *History of Great Britain* (1611), distorts the account considerably, and could be said to have influenced the perspective of the battle reflected in histories of the seventeenth century, such as those of Baker (1643) and Sandford (1677).[43] A review of Speed's corruptions in his *History* is instructive. On the matter of Richard's nightmare before the battle, Speed refers to dreams 'nightly' experienced even before he reached Bosworth. He elaborates on the orations and provides sample opinions of the ordinary soldiers after hearing Richard's speech. Lord Stanley is said to join the battle on Henry's side at the start, and Richard's precipitate move is said merely to be made 'from the range of his owne battell'.[44] The personal combat between the two chief commanders is given lurid emphasis: 'Richmond ... most lion like coped with this cruell Bore, and held him maugre his tuskes at his sword point.'[45] According to Speed, a horse is brought to the king, offering him an escape whilst he is fighting in the thick of the *melée*. This is a contraction of events neither in Hall nor Holinshed. Indeed, Vergil's use of the word *descendit* may imply the contrary.[46] Speed also adds a piece about the victorious army being given leave to take the spoils of the field; and he is also the first to change the *Great Chronicle's* pursuivant of Arms 'Norrey' to one called 'Blanc Sent Leger'.[47] But above all Speed's sequence of events is untrustworthy. The nightmares are said to be *before* Richard reaches the field; George Stanley is said to be on the point of execution *before* the armies are engaged; King Richard is said to be drawing up his line of battle at the time the encounter is about to commence; and there is ambiguity over the sequence of who passes the marsh.

Plate 3. A detail from John Speed's map of Leicestershire of 1610, showing his insertion of 'Red More' within the area of 'Kinge Richards feild'. (Compare with Smith's map, overleaf.)

One major corruption in Speed had a determining effect on ideas about the site of the battle which were to emerge in the antiquarian 'rediscovery' of the eighteenth century. In Speed's words, King Richard 'marched toward the enemy, and upon a faire plaine called *Redmore* neere unto *Bosworth* about seven miles west from *Leicester* he pitched downe his Tents.'[48] Here Speed confuses the site of the encampment with the site of the battle, a point established already by Holinshed, whose *Chronicle* records that Richard pitched his field 'on a hill called Anne Beame'.[49] Even Hall in the 1540s drew a clear distinction between the encampment and the 'plain', into which the army marched 'out of there camp'.[50]

Speed's *Atlas and Theatre of Great Britain* of 1611 was also popular and influential; it illustrated the English counties in large annotated maps.[51] On his map of Leicestershire (1610), Speed placed 'Kinge Richards feild' (first established by the cartographer Saxton in 1576) in a diagonal axis on either side of the Sence brook, but inscribed the name 'Red More' north of the stream. In so doing, he further endorsed a false notion about the existence of 'Redmore Plain'; it came to be thought that this area of the battle was in the parish of Sutton Cheney (north of the Sence) and that the 'red-' element in the name had an adjectival function and referred to red soil. It is important to stress from the start, therefore, that the name is not included either on Saxton's original map of the county nor on the important emendation by Smith of 1602; and, furthermore, that the name 'Redmore' is a corruption of *Redemore*, the original name for the battle, and which was in fact spelt correctly in the decorative inset on Speed's map.[52] Speed's maps are attractive and interesting examples of early cartography, but they must be treated with caution; their many errors detract from their validity as historical documents.

Finally, having mentioned the extent to which Shakespeare reflected a common oral tradition which was partly separate from the chronicle record, it is worth noting that manuscripts of songs which incorporate that tradition survive from the time when Stow and Speed were writing their histories, but which could be said to diverge from their understanding of the event.

Plate 4. Detail from Smith's
map of Leicestershire and
Rutland (augmented by
William Burton), 1602,
showing
'K. Ric: feild'.

Courtesy of Leicestershire Museums,
Arts and Records Service

The songs make up the corpus of the Stanley ballads, the earliest manuscript of which – Harley 542 – was copied by Stow before 1568, and exists amongst his collection.[53] This account corresponds to that in the ballad called *Bosworth Feilde* which survives among the Percy manuscripts in a version of the first quarter of the seventeenth century.[54] It is agreed, however, that its original composition was much earlier, and that the material from which it is derived may well date from before 1495.[55] In the case of the ballad called *Ladye Bessiye*, also among the Percy manuscripts, one version – Harley 367 – dates from about 1600, and another version from the time of Charles II.[56] Again, the material upon which it is based, whilst possibly to be differentiated from that of the *Bosworth Feilde* ballad, is very likely to have originated in this form before 1500, but possibly after Sir William Stanley's execution in 1495.[57]

The importance of these ballads is that they reflect an oral tradition, albeit poetically rendered, which is well-informed and near-contemporary. They are based possibly on knowledgeable witnesses within the Stanley party at the battle, and provide details which endorse the account by Polydore Vergil. This material was very likely common knowledge throughout the sixteenth century, communicated by songsters and balladeers, and assimilated by Shakespeare. In the account of the battle I give, it will feature largely, together with Polydore Vergil, as an authoritative source.

CHAPTER TWO

Eighteenth and Nineteenth Century Antiquarian Interpretations

The eighteenth century saw a resurgence of interest in the battle of Bosworth which ever since has given rise to acute problems of interpretation. Eighteenth century antiquarianism differed from the historiographical interest occasioned by the founding of the Society of Antiquaries in 1572. In fact, it is generally agreed that antiquarian scholarship began to decline after 1730 when ideals of empirical analysis were increasingly abandoned.[1]

A representative figure of the age was Horace Walpole, to whom the Middle Ages were 'a bric-à-brac shop from which he could pick out material for an elegant (and inaccurate) historical essay'.[2] His *Historic Doubts on the Reign of Richard III* (1768), one of the early attempts to rehabilitate the man Richard III, was a challenging polemical statement, although wholly superficial.[3] William Hutton's book *The Battle of Bosworth-Field* (1788) was a direct heir; and we will need therefore to examine Hutton's book, and the influence it has exerted on Bosworth studies.

William Hutton was a self-made Birmingham paper-merchant who held a pragmatic view of authorship. His books were sometimes written as part of a financial and commercial strategy connected with his paper business, although no doubt in response to a genuine interest in antiquities.[4] His autobiography, edited from his diaries by his daughter Catherine Hutton, describes only one brief visit to the site of the battle of Bosworth before he began work on his book. This was in 1770 on his return from visiting relations in Mountsorrel.[5] His treatment by the inhabitants of Market Bosworth on that occasion remained a sore memory for many years.[6]

Hutton's book was popular and influential, but the contemporary remarks of John Throsby, the hard-headed author of the *Select Views in Leicestershire*, are a sobering reminder of its value then as now: 'Hutton has given us "Bosworth fight" in novel and entertaining words, but they are words of conjecture.'[7] Exactly what degree of conjecture can be gathered from Hutton's own comments regarding his sources and methods of enquiry. These were three-fold: visits, folklore and books.

Apart from personal visits of the kind already referred to, Hutton 'made many enquiries into the tradition in the vicinity of Bosworth field, and found these the most copious source of intelligence.'[8] However, these were attended with problems, for in the Preface we read that he had 'more than once put a whole family into silent amazement... by opening a subject, which though

Plate 5. The plan of the battle which William Hutton incorporated in his 1788 book, *The Battle of Bosworth-Field*. It shifts the putative area of 'King Richard's Field' wholly north of the Sence Brook (called here the Tweed).

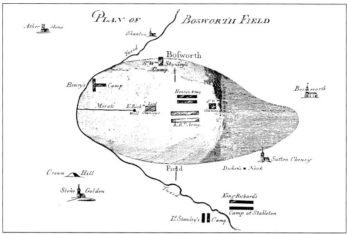

constantly under the eye, they had never noticed.'[9] The local population, we are told, were not always informative: their remarks could be 'crude' and 'contradictory'.[10] Furthermore, archaeological specimens from the area (which Hutton referred to as 'the rubbish of antiquity') were of little help, 'so cankered with the rust of time, as to baffle the judgement'.[11] 'Authentic information of so remote a period,' Hutton concluded, 'is produced with as much difficulty by the antiquary as waters in Arabian deserts by the traveller.'[12]

Hutton's third mode of enquiry were books, and he lists in his Preface 'Hollingshed (*sic*), Grafton, Buck, Dugdale, Rapin, Carte, Walpole and Fenn'.[13] Of these, the chronicle tradition is represented only by Holinshed and Grafton, but in the whole of Hutton's book there seems to be only one quotation (misquoted) from Holinshed, to the effect that the marsh between the two armies was drained by cultivation. This information, however, is discounted by Hutton, who says 'there neither is, nor ever was [a marsh].'[14]

Essentially, it is with Hutton's book that many of the spurious 'traditions' concerning the battle of Bosworth originate, together with much of the misunderstanding about the site of the battle. A selection of Hutton's suppositions, which cannot be substantiated in any source before or contemporary with him, may be listed briefly:

- Camps of the respective commanders at Elmesthorpe, Stapleton (the Bradshaws), Gamble's Close, and 'Whitemoors' (and evidence for the construction of earthworks).[15]
- A quadrangular battle-formation on the summit of Ambion Hill.[16]

- The contrast in the colours of the soil between 'Redmoors' and 'White-moors'.
- The identification of 'King Richard's Field' with 'Redmoor Plain'.
- King Richard's oration in a place called 'Dicken's-nook'.
- The supposed fine weather indicated by 'dust' on the ground.[17]
- Henry Tudor's attack uphill against the king's forces.[18]
- The Stanley forces positioned on either side of the battlefield.
- The conjectural time of day (11 o'clock).[19]
- The king's death at the foot of Ambion Hill, 'near Amyon Lays'
- The southward rout to Stoke Golding, where hollows were supposed to mark the grave-pits of soldiers.[20]
- The 'authority' of local folklore, such as the river running red with blood, the naming of Hollow Meadow (Stoke Golding) from the 'hollaing' of the victorious soldiers, and the secreting of the king's crown under a bush by a common soldier.[21]

These conjectures about the battle of Bosworth, it must be stressed, do not coincide with evidence from earlier sources, some of which were unknown to Hutton and his contemporaries.

One of the chief mistakes which originated with Hutton was the belief that a hill – Ambion Hill – and not a plain was the site of the encounter. This arose from a misunderstanding of Hall's phrase: 'Kyng Richard... marched to a place mete for twoo battayles to encountre by a village called Bosworth... and there he pitched hys felde, refreshed his souldioures & toke his rest.'[22] A significant interpolation in Holinshed is the first mention of Ambion Hill in connection with the battle of Bosworth: 'and there he pitched his field on a hill called Anne Beame, refreshed hys Souldiours and tooke his rest.'[23] Holinshed, reflecting known military practice, was clearly referring to the site of Richard III's encampment, information endorsed by William Burton in his manuscript version of *The Description of Leicestershire*.[24] Indeed, Hall's reference to 'pitching' in association with 'rest' and 'refreshment', implies exactly this. However, Hutton took 'field' in this instance to mean 'battle', and therefore concluded that the battle was fought on a hill called 'Anne Beame'. The term 'field' underwent a marked change of meaning in the early to mid sixteenth century, and especially in its use by sixteenth century chroniclers;[25] but the eighteenth century antiquaries understood 'field' to mean 'battle' because of the standard usage of the expression in this sense in antiquarian writings of the previous century. 'The field of Bosworth' appeared in the sixteenth century London chronicles,[26] and of course 'King Richard's Field' had appeared on a number of maps of Leicestershire since Saxton. Hutton compounded the error by assuming that the place called 'Redmore' was synonymous with 'King Ric: feld' on the early maps, and that this had as its centre Ambion Hill. 'Redmore Plain' therefore came to incorporate Ambion Hill, despite the fact that Ambion is not a plain, nor even, technically, a moor.[27] The plan of the battlefield that Hutton provided in his book endorsed these misunderstandings further by outlining an ovoid area, presumably corresponding with the place called 'King Ric: feld', in a region wholly north of the Sence brook. This does not accord, however, with Smith's 1602 correction of Saxton's map, the earliest devoted solely to the county, which shows 'King Ric: feld' to be equally north and south of the Sence brook.[28]

Hutton was keen to give explanations, and the reasons he gives for 'Redmore' being the name of the battle was that it was descriptive of the colour of the soil on Ambion. His interpretation of the element 'red-' as referring to the colour was possibly inspired by a pun in Michael Drayton's poem *Poly-Olbion:*

> O *Red-more*, it then seem'd, thy name was not in vaine,
> When with a thousands blood, the earth was coloured red. [29]

— which has poetic licence to justify it, as also an allusion perhaps to the symbolic contrast between 'red' and 'white' established very early in connection with the Wars of the Roses.[30] Hutton appropriated the symbolism of 'red' and 'white' *via* his use of the name 'Whitemoors' for the meadows to the west of Ambion:

> Its real name is *Redmoor Plain*, from the colour of the soil; as the meadows on the west are called *White-moors* for the same reason.[31]

In displacing the site of King Richard's camp from Ambion and substituting in its place the site of the battle, Hutton was thereby forced to conjecture other possible camp-sites. Alfred Burne rightly said that Hutton found encampments wherever he detected earthworks, whether they were field-boundaries or natural features.[32] Such are the supposed 'earthworks' at the Bradshaws Farm in Stapleton parish, and on the west of Ambion Hill (Henry's camp, according to Hutton).[33] However, Hutton mistakes the dates of the king's movements from Nottingham and Leicester, and therefore the time required in order to throw up earthworks. Richard III's army left Leicester on 21 August 1485, as the *Crowland Chronicle* records, and reached Ambion later that day.[34] At Ambion, the king found a natural defensive position, augmented by vestigial banks and closes surviving from the medieval deserted village site abandoned before 1400.[35]

The site of 'Dicken's nook' is another dubious tradition that originated with Hutton. Hutton's description of the formation of King Richard's battle-line and the position of this feature from where the king is said to have delivered his oration (north-east or south-east of the battle-line?) is overtly ambiguous.[36] The map by John Pridden in Nichols' *History and Antiquities of Leicestershire* attempts to distinguish the site, and in so doing confuses a 'nook' with a mound, and places a mound where there is no evidence of one ever having existed.[37] What seems to have happened is that Hutton mistook his local informants, for there was indeed a 'Dicken's Nook' in existence behind Sutton Hall in the 1780s, although then (1784) only recently carved out of a larger field called 'Dicken's Close'. This in turn was very likely to have been an eighteenth century enclosure, the name of which perhaps exploited corruptions of the words 'dick' and 'pick', and their variants, which occur in the names of furlongs in the open field south-east of Sutton village. The great field here was known as 'Pick Meadow Field' in the eighteenth century.[38]

Another of the principal misunderstandings in Hutton's interpretation of the battle concerns the salient topographical feature agreed on by three of the primary sources – the marsh. Hutton, confusingly, denies its existence at the same time as describing a 'morass' on the southern slopes of Ambion Hill which Henry Tudor kept on his right.[39] However, Hutton also identifies 'wet' terrain on the north side of Ambion, and it is here that he places the death of the king. This is necessary in order thereby to accommodate his theoretical positioning of Sir William Stanley's army on the north side of the battlefield according to a quadrangular battle formation which Hutton devised.[40]

The 'morass' on the southern slopes of Ambion Hill has presented problems for historians. Gairdner, for example, recognised the problematic nature of Hutton's assertion that the 'swamp where [King Richard] fell [had] become firm land' in 1807, when Holinshed had already said the same in 1577 ('ther was a great marresse there (but at this present by reason of diches cast it is growen to be firme ground)...').[41] Burne, however, insisted that bogs can break out on sloping ground where drainage is left neglected; and having inspected the locality, he concluded that Hutton was correct in placing the marsh here.[42] However, it is not generally understood that a medieval arable field system underlies the wood on the south side of Ambion Hill; and that this implies the cultivation of crops probably at the time the hamlet on Ambion was flourishing in the thirteenth century.[43] Clearly this precludes the likelihood of any natural marshland on Ambion Hill, let alone one sufficiently dangerous or extensive to divert an army. In fact, the presence of water-sodden soil on the south of Ambion is explained by simple geological factors, involving the height of the water-table below the sand-and-gravel cap of the hill. There are several springs on Ambion (one of which came later to be known as King Richard's Well)[44] and those on the south form streams which drain into the Sence brook on the parish boundary of Shenton and Dadlington. Without the aid of channelling, the springs tend to form small pockets of water and swamp. Water also collects in the furrows of the field-strips which, because they lie at right angles to the gradient rather than along it, do not drain excess water. Hutton, who in the 1780s was repeatedly 'set fast in the mire' when examining the wood, could well have been standing on medieval ridge-and-furrow.[45]

Hutton's interpretation of the battle of Bosworth, because of its comprehensive exposition in book form, was the most influential of the late eighteenth century antiquarian reconstructions, but it was not an isolated one. In 1789 John Throsby wrote that

> Opinions are various respecting the positions of the armies at Bosworth Fight; some of them are plausible but without authority to support them [...] Mr. Robinson, of Hinckley, perhaps properly has brought even the Sun in aid of his opinions; and my friend, Mr. Nichols in his Collections, seems transported, beyond his usual gravity, where he describes his visit to this what he calls 'classic ground'.[46]

John Robinson was a dilettante scholar and friend of Nichols and produced a 'Map of the County Five Miles Around Hinckley' in 1785. It was published in Nichols' book, together with an accompanying note.[47] In this he explained that the 'tender ground' where it is said the king's horse was mired was on 'the side next Hinckley', and on the other side of the wood was King Richard's Well: 'The Ambion is supposed to be the place of engagement; but there are many opinions of the position of the line of battle.'[48] The 'tender ground' which represented the traditional 'bog' in which Richard was killed is presumably that shown on John Pridden's map of 1789 which accompanied Nichols' article.[49] Pridden's map was drawn up as a result of an excursion he made with John Nichols and David Wells of Burbage to the locality on 17 July 1789. On the same day he sketched the hall at Sutton Cheney; and the

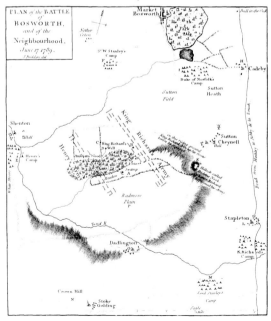

Plate 6. The plan of the battle drawn by John Pridden (1789) for Nichols' *History and Antiquities of Leicestershire* IV (1811). Its mixture of topographical errors and antiquarian invention had an extraordinary influence on the perception of the battle of Bosworth well into the twentieth century.

adventures of the outing are recalled vividly in a letter sent by Nichols to Wells on 31 March 1790.[50]

Pridden's was a more influential map than either Hutton's or Robinson's partly because of its incorporation in Nichols' vast book, but it is important to take note of its confusions and inaccuracies. The explanatory key which Nichols provided mistakes Ambion Hill (marked as 'M' on the map) with the present Harper's Hill in Stapleton, and elevates Dicken's Nook to a hillock along the Dadlington Lane.[51] The Dadlington to Shenton road is omitted, and the Sence brook incorrectly related to the topography. Nor does the hachuring correspond to the landscape relief. Apart from these obvious geographical inaccuracies, Pridden basically follows Hutton and Robinson in placing two opposing battalions on a north-east to south-west axis across Ambion Hill, but indicates nothing of the position or movements of the other armies involved – Northumberland's, Sir William Stanley's and Lord Thomas Stanley's – nor indeed of contingent forces such as those of Norfolk and Oxford. The cartographical details of the map reinforce its assumptions. Pridden illustrated the wood on Ambion and the elongated meadow to the south of it – a meadow called Small Meadow in the eighteenth century surveys of Sutton Cheney.[52] The 'swamp' in this meadow is referred to as the place where it is said King Richard's horse was 'mired,' and certainly wet patches, caused by the alluvial bed of an old stream, are still detectable north of the Ashby canal. But the principal confusion here in relation to the battle is that this 'morass' is on the opposite side of the hill to that where Hutton's Richard was supposedly 'mired' and killed.

Overall, our conclusion can only be that all three maps – Hutton's, Robinson's and Pridden's – vis à vis the battle of Bosworth, are seriously flawed geographically, and cannot act as a basis for the superimposition of a battle 'scenario'. In fact, they illustrate well the difficulties involved in superimposing a medieval battle on a contemporary map.

Nichols' documentation of the evidence for the battle of Bosworth was extensive and important for its time, but in some vital respects it was seriously flawed. He opens by quoting from Burton's annotation to *The Description of Leicestershire* of 1622, but omits to point out that the long second paragraph of the quotation refers, not to Bosworth, but to Ambion, for it was here that Burton wrote 'King Ric: 3 ... the night before the battaile pitched here his tentes'.[53] Nichols also provides relevant quotations from the letters of King Richard from the Harley 433 manuscript up to the time of the battle, and cites too some of the references in the York municipal records quoted in Francis Drake's history of York, *Eboracum*, of 1736.[54] However, 'Redemore' (which Drake gives correctly) is mis-spelt 'Redmore', thus compounding further the etymological confusion concerning this word (see Chapter Three). Apart from one important account of the battle from a primary source – the first printing of the Harley 542 manuscript[55] – Nichols is erratic with his medieval and sixteenth century sources. For example, when he quotes from the chronicle tradition, it is only from Holinshed. In fact, he relies unquestioningly on Hutton's timescale of events, position of camps and topographical associations, which he uses to explain the map by Pridden. In addition, he quotes from Drayton's *Poly-Olbion* and also Sir John Beaumont's poem 'Bosworth Field' first published in 1629.[56] Finally, there are two pages of notes to accompany the map and two plates of illustrations, one of which is headed 'Curiosities found in Bosworth Field',[57] (see Appendix One).

When Nichols wrote in his entry for Sutton Cheney that 'this lordship is celebrated for containing within its boundaries, the noted *Redmore Plain,* whereon Richard the Third lost his crown, his kingdom, and his life'[58] he was not only going well beyond Burton – who mentioned the battle only under Market Bosworth and Dadlington – but also beyond his own analysis in *The History and Antiquities of Hinckley* (1782), which (significantly) pre-dated Hutton. In that book, Nichols reflected what was probably a more accurate contemporary understanding of the site of the battle. From Crown Hill in Stoke Golding, he said, was obtained 'a fine and extensive view along the vale towards Bosworth, being the celebrated ground commonly called King Richard's Field.' It 'comprehended part of those several lordships [Shenton, Sutton, Dadlington and Stoke] when uninclosed.'[59]

However, Nichols' remarks under Sutton Cheney were decisive for shifting the plain of 'Redmore' onto the higher ground and into Sutton parish.

Plate 7. William Burton's manuscript insertion in his copy of *The Description of Leicestershire* (1622) under the entry on Anbein: *'At this place King Rich: 3 ... the night before the battaile pitched here his tentes.'*
Courtesy of Staffordshire Record Office.

All Trades Directories after 1846 include remarks on the battle of Bosworth under Sutton Cheney.[60] Hutton's book too had a wide readership in the nineteenth century through its second edition, reprinted and augmented by Nichols in 1813. James Hollings, a Leicestershire lawyer-turned-historian, clearly had Hutton's scenario in mind when he tracked down the Sandeford (the site of King Richard's death) to a crossing of the Sutton brook on the north-west side of Ambion Hill. 'The place is precisely where we should expect to find it, on a consideration of the relative positions occupied by the rival armies,' he remarks in his letter to *Notes and Queries* of 1858.[61] Exactly – if one accepts Hutton's supposition that Richard was killed to the north of the hill. James Gairdner in his *Archaeologia* article of 1896 adopted Hollings' idea about the positioning of the Sandeford without demur, despite the flaws in Hollings' case;[62] and through Gairdner the belief that the Sandeford is accurately located has been adopted in recent times and presented to the public as a historical 'fact' in an official interpretation of the battle.[63]

On the whole, local writers have long been mesmerised, but also puzzled, by the maps and scenarios provided by these eighteenth century antiquaries. H.J. Francis' manuscript notebook on the battle of Bosworth (now in Hinckley public library) is a case in point. Francis was the first local historian to recognise the confusion in Hollings' geographical knowledge of the area, when he queried Gairdner's placing the Leicester to Atherstone road to the north of Ambion Hill.[64] The archaeologist A.J. Pickering in his own comments on the locality also drew attention to the manifest confusions in Hutton's topographical associations, noted by Gairdner.[65] Daniel Williams in his 1973 battlefield handbook likewise assumes Hollings' notion about the Sandeford to be correct, and furthermore extends the marsh across the Sutton to Dadlington road, but without authority.[66] Williams is alone, moreover, in positioning both Stanley forces north of the battle, but he gives no evidence for this conjecture.[67]

The general public has thus largely been given an impression of the battle of Bosworth based on flawed eighteenth and nineteenth century ideas and on long entrenched but traceable corruptions of evidence going back to the mid-sixteenth century. It is clear that none of the explanations of the battle of Bosworth that we find in authors as diverse as Kendall and Ross, Burne and Williams, can be trusted, and that therefore a new assessment of the evidence is needed. Recent work by Goodman, Richmond, Harris, Griffiths and Thomas has pointed the way;[68] whilst my own contribution has largely been devoted to an examination of the data related specifically to the site of the battle.[69] In the following chapter we will explore this aspect of the argument, whilst in Chapter Four will be offered a new interpretation of the battle based upon a fresh assessment of the primary sources.

CHAPTER THREE
Hill, Plain and Marsh:
The Topography of a Battle

The Leicestershire historian, William Burton, is a reliable authority for the corpus of information that was available locally in the late sixteenth and early seventeenth centuries. He was collecting data for his book *The Description of Leicestershire* from c.1597 onwards, having spent his childhood at Lindley near the Watling Street.[1] His family were lords of the manor of Dadlington and Higham, bordering the battlefield, and it is in his entry on Dadlington that he records the burials from the battle at Dadlington church, and the fact that the village 'lay neere unto the place where King Richard his field was fought'.[2] There is no other mention of the battle of Bosworth in Burton except under Bosworth itself, since Burton's avowed aim was not to write history – which was 'the least part of the book' – but to concentrate on antiquities, genealogy and heraldry.[3] His entry on Bosworth is therefore significant, not only for what it chooses to say but for its unequivocal nature:

> Not that this field was fought at this place (it being fought in a large, flat, plaine, and spacious ground, three miles distant from this Towne [Bosworth], between the Towne of *Shenton, Sutton, Dadlington, and Stoke*:) but for that this Towne was the most worthy towne of note neere adiacent, and was therefore called *Bosworth field.*[4]

Burton provides three pieces of evidence for his siting of the battle. The first, concerning a 'little Mount cast up', must be ignored since Burton gives no exact location and only associates it with 'common report' concerning Richmond's oration to his army. The other evidence, however, is more reliable. Burton records that at the enclosure of Stoke Golding (in c.1600) 'divers peeces of armor, weapons and other warlike accoutrements' were dug-up. Many of the arrow-heads 'of a long, large and big proportion, farre greater then any now in use' came into his possession at the time.[5]

That artefacts were dug up in the vicinity of Stoke Golding and not, for example, in the vicinity of either Bosworth or Cadeby (where enclosure was also taking place from the late sixteenth century onwards)[6] is in itself significant, but that such a large quantity is recorded is persuasive of the fact that we have here evidence of a location for a principal part of the battle of Bosworth. The enclosure Burton refers to was initiated by Lord Harrington of Exton shortly before the sale of the lordship of Stoke Golding to his tenant farmers.[7] Part of that enclosure involved the draining of wetland between Stoke and Dadlington, and the assarting of areas of heath and 'fen holes' in the western half of the parish. It is here no doubt that this debris was discovered.

The third fragment of evidence provided by Burton is that of oral report: 'by relation of the inhabitants, who have many occurrences and passages yet fresh in memory'.[8] It would appear that Burton misses a generation when referring to local folk 'which saw the battaile fought' living within less than forty years: but it is nevertheless highly likely that Burton would have met and spoken with inhabitants of these villages whose parents and grandparents were witnesses to the events of 1485.

We have seen how the notion that the battle of Bosworth was fought on a 'plaine' – corroborated by Burton – is first to be found in a casual phrase in Hall's *Chronicle*, though not in Vergil. However, this notion does seem to reflect the topographical picture that emerges from the ballads: that the battle was fought on low-lying ground in a 'vale', surrounded by hills. Both ballad traditions mutually endorse certain specific geographical details. Thus the ballad called *Bosworth Feilde* suggests that Sir William Stanley and Lord Thomas Stanley were not far from each other on the same side of the battlefield and positioned on hilltops. The Harley 542 manuscript implies that both Stanley forces 'removyd to a hyghe mountayne', whilst the *Bosworth Feilde* ballad states that only Sir William Stanley did.[9] However, his brother is presumably deemed to be on a hill, since

> King Richard looked on the mountaines hye,
> & sayd, 'I see the banner of the Lord Stanley'[10]

This detail appears to be borne out by a line in the *Ladye Bessiye* tradition, where Lord Stanley, leaving the battle to his brother, decided to 'hove on this hill/ That faire battell for to see'.[11] Sir William Stanley's position on a hill is further substantiated by the reference in Harley 542 that he came 'downe at a banke' to set upon Richard prior to the king's death.[12]

If the Stanleys were on hills, so too it appears was the king – in the early stages of the battle at least, since the Harley 367 version of *Ladye Bessiye* describes King Richard 'hoving' upon the mountaine aware of the banner of the 'boulde Standley'.[13] Obviously, there is a variation in emphasis here, but taken together with other clues (such as the word *descendit* from Polydore Vergil), we might plausibly conjecture that the king watched the progress of the battle from the vantage-point of a hill (which might well have been Ambion) before he made his move against Henry Tudor.

More significant perhaps is the description of King Richard's army occupying lower ground in 'a dale of [....] myles coompasse'.[14] The *Bosworth Feilde* ballad in referring to Sir William Stanley's removal to a hilltop, reads as follows:

then he removed unto a mountaine full hye,
& looked into a dale ffull dread;
5 miles compasse, no ground they see,
ffor armed men & trapped steeds.

theyr armor glittered as any gleed;
in 4 strong battells they cold fforth bring;
they seemed noble men att need
as ever came to maintaine [a] King[15]

Both ballad traditions mention the hill upon which Henry Tudor was crowned – the 'mountayne hyghe' to which the victors withdrew – whilst *Ladye Bessiye* also refers to a hill to which the Duke of Norfolk retreated during the battle. Here he met his death at the hands of Sir John Savage ('he went up to a wind-mill,/ & stood upon a hill soe hye,/ there he mett Sir John Savage, a valyant Knight...').[16]

The ballad sources, therefore, do illustrate something of the geography of the battle, notwithstanding their poetic character. As with many of the sources they are suspect on a number of calculable issues, but probably not on the nature of the battlefield terrain. Their advantage over some other sources is the intimate perspective they provide deriving very possibly from a participating source. They suggest clearly that both Stanleys positioned themselves on hills, that Richard III also watched from the vantage-point of a hill and that the armies occupied a 'dale'. The question remains, is the 'dale' referred to in the Harley 542 manuscript the same as the 'plain' described by Hall and Burton, and what connection has this with the *Redemore* after which the battle was named?

As to the first identification, it would seem likely that within the area of 'King Ric: feld' as marked on Saxton's 1576 map of Leicestershire and Warwickshire, the only terrain which can conceivably be described as both a 'dale' and 'plain' is the low-lying landscape, never much more than 285 feet, which lies to the west of the line of the hills on which Ambion, Sutton Cheney, Dadlington and Stoke Golding stand. However, of far more significance is the identification of at least part of this area with the Redemore proper, and I wish now to consider the etymology of this name, which has already been referred to in previous chapters.

The earliest mention of Redemore in connection with the battle of Bosworth is in itself an important piece of primary evidence. It occurs among the clerk's minutes taken down in the council chamber of York from information imparted by emissaries specially sent to the battlefield of Bosworth in order to report on events.[17] On 16 August 1485 one John Sponer, sergeant to the mace of the mayor and aldermen of the city of York, together with others, was sent to King Richard at Nottingham to receive his 'pleysure' as to mustering forces within York 'for the subduying of his ennemyes late arrivyed in the parties of Walles'.[18] By the 19th, one of the party, John Nicholson, had returned to York, the report being entered in the minute book that Nicholson had come from Beskwood, the royal lodge near Nottingham, and that eighty armed men were to be sent 'in all hast possible' to the king, under John Hastinges, gentlemen to the mace.[19] It would therefore seem likely that Sponer remained with the king's people at Nottingham and then at Leicester, for it is he who returned to York on the 23rd, the day after the battle, to report the grave and dramatic news of the king's death:

> It was shewed by diverse personnes, and especially by John Sponer, send unto the feld of Redemore to bring tidinges frome the same to the Citie, that King Richard, late mercifully reigning upon us, was [....] pitiously slane and murdred, to the grete hevynesse of this Citie.[20]

Whether or not John Sponer was at the battlefield itself or remained in Leicester, there can be no doubt that his information provides the most direct link we have with the battle. In all likelihood Sponer rode through the night of the 22nd to reach York on the 23rd in time for the council assembled customarily in the afternoon. The 'diverse personnes' may have been the remnants of the York soldiery who were sent, undoubtedly by horse, the previous week.[21] The council clerk solemnly recorded a Latin memorandum on folio 169 of the York City House Book to the effect that the battle was fought *apud Redemore juxta Leicestre*.[22]

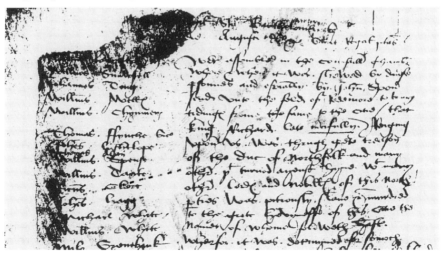

Plate 8. The earliest record of the battle of Bosworth, 23 August 1485: York House Book 2–4, 169v. *'John Sponer, send unto the feld of Redemore to bring tidinges frome the same to the Citie ...'*
By permission of York City Archives

From the time the battle of Bosworth was fought until well into the sixteenth century it was known as 'Redemore' or 'Redesmore'. Clearly, the information Sponer possessed, so close to the event, confirms that the place where the armies met, in a remote corner of south-west Leicestershire, was a moorland known by that name to the inhabitants and to the participants. The variation 'Redesmore' occurs in a near-contemporary collection of notes made by London merchants, now in the College of Arms.[23] That and a further reference in a marginal note in a copy of Fabyan's *Chronicle* of 1533, now in the National Library of Scotland (see p.13), is confirmation of the likely etymological derivation from the genitive-plural of the Anglo-Saxon word for 'reed', *hrēodes*.[24] Consequently, we are dealing with a moorland incorporating or adjacent to an area of wetland – no doubt identical to the marsh mentioned in Polydore Vergil and the Harley 542 manuscript.

It has been argued that there were a variety of names for the battle of Bosworth at the time it was fought.[25] This, however, is debatable, for none of the alternatives may be considered to be as authoritative as Sponer's report. The name 'Bosworth' did not emerge until twenty-five years after the event, when it occurs in documents and was used by Vergil. Its first printing is in fact in the 1516 edition of Fabyan's *Chronicle*, where *Bellum de bosworth* is printed in the margin.[26] It was not uncommon for battles during the Wars of the Roses to be given various names before one eventually became universally accepted. The battle of Towton (1461), for example, was called both Northfield and Palme Sunday field in successive accounts.[27] This is partly because such battles, when the encounter was premeditated, were unlikely to have been fought near to settlements; invariably an area of waste moorland or heath was sought between townships and on the margins of parishes, and this is undoubtedly true of Bosworth. Furthermore, without an immediately recognisable or significant location, annals and reports tended to contrive their own references. The Crowland chronicler – to whom the battle was *bellum Mirivallense* – may have wished to draw attention to the part played by the abbot of Merevale in the victory of Henry Tudor.[28] (King Richard is likewise described as camping 'eight miles from Leicester near to Merevale Abbey').[29] John Rous's location of the battle on the Warwickshire–Leicestershire border is also understandable in the light of Rous's Warwickshire connections.[30] One other intriguing reference, however, occurs in a genealogy of Henry VII found among a bundle of scientific notes once in the possession of Humphrey Lluyd, and now in the Bodleian Library.[31] Here the battle is referred to as 'Brownehethe', and it has been suggested that this may be a re-translation from the Welsh *rhos goch* ('red moor').[32] An association with heathland is certainly common to the various early mentions of the battle.

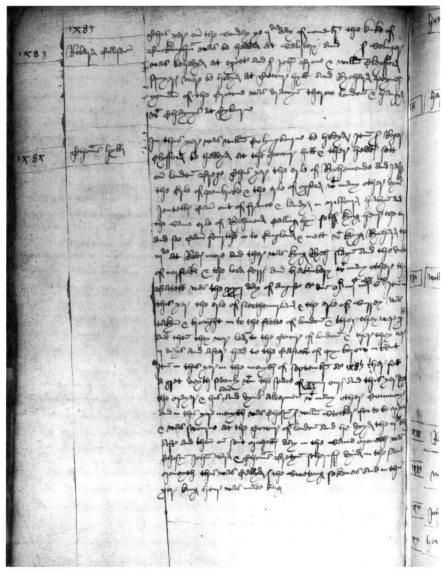

Plate 9. The 'Londoner's Notes' MS., College of Arms MS 2 M6
'... *the same erle of Rychmond calling hym selff Kyng Henry the vii ... camm*
fourthe into Einglond and mett with Kyng Rychard the iiide att Redesmore...'

By permission of the College of Arms.

Clearly, then, the name Redemore suggests the kind of wetland which several of the primary sources for the battle of Bosworth show to have been a major topographical factor; and we are further persuaded that a place called Redemore did indeed exist within the area later designated as 'King Ric: feld'. A hitherto unnoticed document – an agreement about the allocation of tithes in the parish of Hinckley and its adjacent chapelries dated 1283 – specifically refers to 'six roods of meadow in *Redemor* in the fields of Dadlington' which the vicar of Hinckley, one Gilbert de Burstall, was allowed to mow and carry away at his own cost.[33] This document, in itself an unusual survival, was drawn up as a result of a dispute that arose between the vicar and the prior of Hinckley, who acted as procurator for the abbey and convent of Lyre in Normandy, to which Hinckley church belonged. The reference to 'Redemor' is important because it is the earliest mention of the name and confirms the etymological derivation I have suggested; it also specifies meadow (*pratum*), and gives an indication as to where it lay – *in campis de Daddington.*[34]

The old chapelry of Dadlington covers an area of just over a thousand acres and lies mainly to the north and west of the village of Dadlington which occupies a hill on its southern fringe. Before enclosure (after 1670), the far west quarter of the chapelry encompassed part of a moorish common (former heathland and waste) divided from the open field on its eastern side by a band of alluvial flatland subject to periodic flooding.[35] This must once have remained open water or marsh for much of the year, fed by streams and springs emerging from the cleft of the hills between Dadlington and Stoke. The excess water would have gradually drained into channels dug specifically to carry it

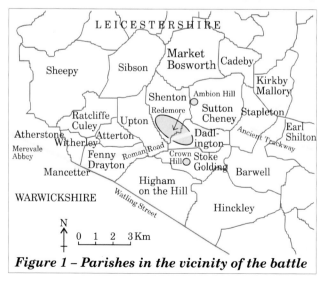

Figure 1 – Parishes in the vicinity of the battle

to the Sence brook near Shenton. It seems likely that drainage channels have been cut periodically since agricultural improvement gained momentum in the sixteenth century at a time of manorial fragmentation; but before that in the fourteenth and fifteenth centuries, when there was depopulation and shrinkage from the margins of the settlements in this part of south-west Leicestershire, management of much of the wetland in Dadlington may have been abandoned.[36] Before the fourteenth century, however, it does seem that the fringes of the wetland were managed as hay-meadows by the inhabitants of the neighbouring vills. Although there are few documentary survivals from an early period, and in consequence we have to reconstruct this landscape to some extent conjecturally, there are clues in the later history of the area which point to this kind of development. For example, a meadow called 'Segwelle hamm' first mentioned in a charter of Robert de Campagnia of c.1250, is locatable from later evidence in the valley between Dadlington and Stoke.[37] The name is suggestive of a water-meadow adjacent to marshland, and of a spring or even a pool formed by the issues and fringed by sedge.[38] The adjacent area in Dadlington chapelry is likely to be the Redemore of 1283 (an area later distinguished by the name of the 'Fenmore closes'),[39] and this name in turn suggests the presence, and possibly the cultivation, of reed-beds for thatching. Parish boundaries often meet in neutral areas, such as waste, heath, wood and marsh;[40] and such a terrain is likely to be indicated by the convergence of the boundaries of Shenton, Dadlington, Stoke and Upton in an area $1^1/_2$ miles west of Dadlington. Parts of the later Upton and Stoke commons met here, whilst the southern boundary of Shenton parish crossed an area called (though only evidenced from later records) the 'Fomers', a name itself indicative of wetland.[41] The slightly cambered region of moorland between the tributaries of the Sence brook in Shenton and Dadlington parishes was known as 'The Great Moor' in the early eighteenth century, no doubt borrowing its name from a much earlier period.[42] The abnormal absence of ridge-and-furrow cultivation in an extensive area of this marginal land suggests that it remained part-meadow, part-moorland from time immemorial, alternating probably between wasteland and heath in times of recession, and grazing common in times of expansion.[43] References to 'heath', 'fennes' and 'fen holes' are found in sixteenth century records for both Stoke Golding and Shenton.[44]

The geological conditions of this part of south-west Leicestershire supports the landscape development I have suggested. Several unusually broad bands of alluvial silt and loam extend south from the Sence brook at Shenton and occupy much of the valley on either side of the Fenn Lanes. Fox-Strangeways in the *Atherstone Memoir* of 1900 describes these areas as being laid down in 'depressions that were formerly lakes and swamps' at the time of the retreat of the ice-cap.[45] It has further been suggested that the gravel terraces along the Sence brook at Shenton (SP 385 996) may have impeded the drainage flow and therefore aided the ponding-up of the vale south of Shenton.[46] There may also be a case for suggesting that the construction of the Roman road in the 1st century A.D. in the form of a causeway across the alluvium at a point called the Fen Meadows was instrumental in ponding-up the area of the later 'Fenmore Closes' to the south, at a period when the Roman road fell out of use. The diversion of the Roman road from its alignment certainly suggests later compromises in the negotiation of the wetland at this point.[47]

The laying-down of 'lacustrine' alluvium is associated only with geographical conditions immediately after the retreat of the ice-cap. Later marshland development results from poor drainage in a valley bottom. The absence of significant deposits of peat in areas which may possibly have been former meres is explained by microbial activity in the silt deposits.[48] Tentative distinctions are sometimes drawn between fens and marshes, a marsh being an area of intermittent standing water occurring on soil, whilst a fen or bog is associated with crucial quantities of peat.[49] The former definition – that of a marsh – distinguishes the area of the Redemore exactly, in that an area of intermittent freshwater marsh is likely to aid the cultivation of valuable and lush meadow grass which would have been mowed twice a year for winter hay (as suggested in the terms of the Hinckley-Lyre Agreement).[50] However, it does appear that there are small quantities of peat and peaty loam, as also of running sand, identifiable in the plain south and west of Ambion Hill, some of them probably corresponding with the 'fen holes' of the sixteenth century documents. These may well have been formed in small pockets of water on the clay fringes of the alluvium. Hollow Meadow is likely to be named after such a 'hole'.[51]

The geology of the general area of 'King Richard's Field' is characterised by the drift deposit mapped as lake clay. This is a brown-grey plastic laminated earth laid down in a northerly arm of 'Lake Harrison', a vast pro-glacial tract of water that once covered much of the west Midlands during the final stages of the second Ice Age.[52] Other deposits of boulder-clay, sand and gravel were laid down when the glaciers retreated; villages and farmsteads usually lie on the fringes of the sand and gravel caps and the boulder-clay. What is noticeable is that Ambion Hill – distinguished as lake clay with a sand cap at the 390 foot contour – is not therefore characterised by red soil since the area of the sand deposit would not formerly have been cultivated. Shades of orange-brown soil in areas to the north of Ambion result from the exposure here of the Mercian Mudstone.[53] The camber of moorish land between the two areas of alluvium on either side of the Fenn Lanes resulted in an 'island' of pasture and heath in the western extremity of Dadlington parish. This was the southern half of the 'Great Moor' described in eighteenth century records relating to Shenton parish.

Plate 10. The site of the battle of Bosworth. Part of the Redemore in the parish of Dadlington, looking SE. The photograph was taken on 24 January 1988, when the meadows adjoining Fenn Lanes (in the foreground) were under flood.
Photograph courtesy of Mr Gordon Webster

What the geological evidence indicates, therefore, is that the only location where a substantial marshland is likely to have existed in the fifteenth century within the area of Saxton's 'King Ric: feld' is in the valley of the tributaries of the Sence brook. This wetland would have been fed by springs between Dadlington and Stoke Golding, and would have developed in the unusually broad band of alluvial silt and loam in the valley. That this is the Redemore of the fifteenth century is strongly suggested by the wording of the Hinckley-Lyre Agreement, and that the surrounding pastures and moor constituted a 'place mete for twoo battayles to encountre' is deduced from the historico-topographical clues of extensive heathland and moorland existing at that time.[54]

There can be little doubt, therefore, that this wetland was the *palus* which Polydore Vergil describes standing between the two armies at the start of the battle; and the fact that the suggested freshwater marsh in this area lies on a north-south axis reconciles the problem of Henry Tudor's manoeuvre leftward out of the direction of the sun. It might also be suggested that this area witnessed the final *melée* of the battle, since the battle is deemed to have ended close to Crown Hill in Stoke Golding. If we accept the detail in Jean Molinet's *Chronicle* that King Richard was killed when his horse stumbled in the marsh, then the death of the king occurred in the region of the Fenn Lanes, possibly in a pocket of water, at a fording-place, and 'upon the plain'.

The surviving reference to the place of King Richard's death – the 'Sandeford' – occurs in a Proclamation issued by Henry VII shortly after the battle. A circular letter was read in the city of York on 24 August 1485, and copied down in the municipal records by the clerk to the council. The original has not survived, but a transcription of it is given by Drake in his *Eboracum* of 1736.[55] The same information – that King Richard was killed at a place called Sandeford (or Sandeforth) in the county of Leicester – is preserved in the Latin Memorandum of 23 August 1485 in folio 169 of the York City House Book.[56] No such named place has been found to exist in the vicinity of 'King Richard's Field', despite Hollings' conjecture of 1858.[57] We are therefore left to surmise as to whether a place called Sandeford did once exist as a location known to the inhabitants by that name, and where it is likely to have been. The name – common among micro-toponyms in medieval records – suggests a fording-place or crossing associated with sand in the geology. Margaret Gelling has shown that the incidence of the '-ford' suffix in place names in the Ock Valley, Berkshire, derives from the occurrence of ancient causeways across former marshland in the flood-plain of the Ock, her view being that the '-ford' name is not here associated with distinctive conventional river or stream crossings.[58] In the area of the Redemore in Dadlington chapelry there is one location to which this theory might apply. The Fenn Lanes, an ancient Roman road, would have crossed an arm of the wetland on a causeway which may in succeeding centuries have become ruined. The distinctive shift in the alignment of the road at this point implies technical difficulties in the fording of the alluvium at a post-enclosure date.[59] The decay of the causeway may have aided the deposit of peat here and added to the treacherous nature of the crossing in periods of neglect. Certainly, peat is evidenced in small quantities adjacent to the Fenn Meadows, and the meadows themselves have pockets of running sand below the soil surface.[60] It might also be significant that the field immediately to the south-east of this crossing was named Sand Pit Close in 1849, although there seems to be no obvious evidence of the existence of a conventional eighteenth or nineteenth century sand-pit.[61] The suggestion therefore is only a tentative one, but such a location would correspond very closely with other clues concerning the situation of the final *melée* of the battle of Bosworth, particularly in view of the fact that the battle must have ended substantially nearer to Stoke Golding and in the valley of Dadlington chapelry.

The significance of the plain to the south and west of Ambion Hill, and consequently of Dadlington chapelry, is confirmed by the existence of a licence issued to the churchwardens of Dadlington and dated 1511, and of a confraternity letter of indulgence printed shortly afterwards. Both these documents have been known to exist for some time, the licence since its first citation in Brewer's 1862 catalogue of *State Letters and Papers of Henry VIII,*[62] but their significance has only recently been understood. What they individually reveal is the important part played by the church and chapelry of Dadlington in the events of 22 August 1485. The Dadlington licence itself provided an alternative name for the battle of Bosworth, 'Dadlyngton field'; its purpose was to licence under royal seal the churchwardens of Dadlington chapel to collect alms in the dioceses of Lincoln, Chester, Worcester and Norwich 'for and towardis the bielding of a chapell of sainte James standing upon a parcell of the grounde where Bosworth feld, otherwise called Dadlyngton feld, in our countie of Leicestr' was done.'[63] It has recently been shown that the expression 'bielding' would indicate repairs and improvements to the existing church of St. James, rather than to a new structure as such. It is highly unlikely that another chapel with the same dedication would have been built within the chapelry, and indeed there are precedents for the use of the term.[64] If this is the case, of course, then the document shows that Dadlington church itself was considered an appropriate building for the battlefield chantry. It therefore seems likely that whatever funds were raised from the appeal contributed to the maintenance of the existing chapel, and some of the fabric of St. James', Dadlington, may be evidence of this.[65] The confraternity letter which was printed after the licence does suggest a significant shift of emphasis in its wording, since the text specifically mentions the maintenance of the chapel and the upkeep of priests to say masses therein for the souls of the slain at the battle. The document is also important for confirming at such an early date that many of the slain

Plate 11. The Dadlington Licence, 24 August 1511: PRO c.82/367.
'... for and towardis the bielding of a chapell of sainte James standing upon a parcell of the grounde where Bosworth feld otherwise called Dadlyngton feld in our countie of Leicester was done.'
By permission of the Public Record Office

Plate 12. The confraternity letter or indulgence printed 1511 x 1518, granting pardon to the benefactors of St. James's chapel, Dadlington, on the establishing there of a chantry to the slain of Bosworth Field. Only two or three copies are known to exist, at Harvard University and the British Library.

from the battle were buried in the vicinity of Dadlington church: '... to ye wheche ye bodyes or bones of the men sleyne in ye seyde feelde beth broght & beryed.'[66]

   In all, then, the documentary evidence from the early sixteenth century, together with a medieval reference to the location of the Redemore in Dadlington parish, places this hamlet and its chapel at the centre of the events of 1485 – a fact which is in stark contrast to the associations which have been held to exist in the neighbouring village of Sutton Cheney. Here, a reputed traditional connection between Richard III and the parish church is only of fairly recent date, since such an association is neither recorded nor evidenced before the 1920s.[67] As Burton later implied, it was Dadlington that was adjacent to the site of the battle, and the fields of Dadlington which provided the original name for it: both 'Dadlyngton feld' and 'the feld of Redemore'.

CHAPTER FOUR
The Battle Of Bosworth:
A New Interpretation

The details of Henry, Earl of Richmond's 'victorious journey' from Milford Haven in Pembrokeshire to the field of Redemore in Leicestershire are contained primarily in Polydore Vergil's *Anglica Historia* and in the somewhat erratic narrative of the Stanley ballads, *Ladye Bessiye* and *Bosworth Feilde*. This material is augmented by a number of contemporary letters and commissions of array, and also by a fair amount of local tradition (much of it of uncertain reliability) still current in the places through which Henry passed.

To give a coherent time-sequence to the journey is not easy, but it does seem that Henry's progress through Wales was slow compared with his progress through England. This is shown by a letter sent from 'beside oure towne of Machen Lloyd' (Machynlleth) to Sir Roger Kynaston and dated 14 August 1485, which Griffiths and Thomas quote in their book *The Making of the Tudor Dynasty*.[1] Previously it had been thought that Henry passed through Machynlleth on the 11th August. Henry's more cautious progress through Wales is accounted for by his need to co-ordinate plans and secure promises of support from the Welsh lords,[2] and also by the difficulties he encountered at Cardigan and Aberystwyth, both with royal garrisons which seem to have resisted his advance. This is given credence in Vergil's manuscript of the *Anglica Historia*, though not in the published version.[3]

According to the ballad tradition, Henry reached Shrewsbury by the 16th August. He was barred entry but by the persuasion of messengers from Sir William Stanley at Stone, the gates were opened and he passed through.[4] The sources and the traditions tell of a number of adventures and set-backs encountered by Henry between Shrewsbury and Atherstone. Vergil, for example, stresses the feelings of trepidation which Henry experienced on this long march.[5] The night he spent away from his soldiers between Lichfield and Tamworth has been taken by one writer to indicate the possibility that Henry was thinking of desertion during the bleakest hour of his journey.[6] Clearly it was in the interests of the Stanleys to continue to support the young pretender, just as it was in Henry's interest to secure assurances along the way. He must have known that he could not win a battle without their aid. True to his character and reputation, Lord Thomas Stanley, Henry's step-father, remained overtly cautious in his commitment to Henry, realising that he had to be seen to be withdrawing in the face of Henry's army in the pretence of shadowing it whilst advancing to the place of battle.[7] The evidence seems to be that both Stanley forces necessarily remained separate until the secret rendezvous at Atherstone on the 20th or 21st of August.

It is clear from the Harley 542 MS version of *Bosworth Feilde* that Henry reached Atherstone by the evening of 20th August.[8] Local tradition records that he spent the night at an inn, the Three Tuns, but it seems more likely that he made use of the nearby Cistercian abbey of Merevale, the major landowner in the area. Henry was later to recompense the abbot of Merevale for 'right gret hurtes, charges, and lossis' done to the house of Merevale 'as in going over his ground, to the destruccioun of his cornes and pastures'.[9] This implies bivouacking in the neighbourhood where Merevale managed demesne farms, and may have covered damages caused by one or other of the Stanley forces who, according to the Harley 542 MS, spent the night in a dale – perhaps the valley of the confluence of the Sence and Anker north of Atherstone itself.[10] Henry, who was already there, seems to have been to the south of the town burgages, among the woods of Merevale. The pattern at Shrewsbury and Lichfield had been to camp outside towns, on hills or heathlands, and to cause as little harm as possible when passing through.[11] The *Bosworth Feilde* ballad also suggests that the meeting between Henry and the Stanleys on Sunday the 21st involved crossing the Anker from the south to the north out of a 'fforrest syde' – the high wooded slopes of Oldbury and Mancetter.[12] In the Harley 78 manuscript there is a list of what may be knights dubbed at this meeting before the battle.[13]

By now the Earl of Richmond knew of the approach of the king's army to its camp site at Ambion. Consequently he would have looked for a suitable place to engage battle and to arrange his formations in the unfamiliar landscape of the Leicestershire-Warwickshire border. To the south, beyond Watling Street, was a wooded country encompassing the fringes of the ancient forest of Arden; to the north, was a bare, rolling upland of isolated and scattered hamlets.[14] Much of this landscape was rough pasture, heath and scrub. There was a tradition in William Burton's family that his ancestor, John Herdwick of Lindley, helped Henry to get 'the advantage of the ground, sun and wind' the night before the battle.[15] This tradition may only be local, but coming from Burton it has good authority, and describes the kind of assistance essential for the tactics of a rebel army.

If we believe the evidence both of the ballad tradition and of Polydore Vergil then it must be assumed that Henry's army (and by implication those of the Stanley brothers) set up camp near to the battlefield on the night of the 21st August.[16] Indeed, the reparations to the villages of Witherley, Mancetter, Atterton and Fenny Drayton suggest the foraging of the army prior to their last encampment, and the fact that Fenny Drayton (together with Atherstone) received the major compensation indicates the direction of the march across the cornfields of the parish.[17] Here the eastern quarter of Fenny Drayton borders the common waste where the boundaries of Upton, Shenton, Dadlington and Stoke meet. The wording of the reparations document is significant in that it specifies 'losses' of corn and grain 'at oure late victorious feld' (thus foraging for use) rather than 'destruccioun' of corns and pastures as in the case of similar documents addressed to Merevale Abbey and resulting from the 'gret repayre and resorte that oure people commyng toward oure late feld' sustained.[18]

The few clues that remain concerning the position of the Stanleys suggest a vantage-point to the south of the battlefield, in which case it is probable that Lord Stanley's army, still appearing to withdraw ahead of Henry's, moved to the spur of hills beyond Higham and Lindley on which the villages of Stoke and Dadlington stand. Stanley's plan had to incorporate an apparent strategy on behalf of the king – an advance-guard shadowing the enemy – and at the same time a manoeuvre which placed him in a position where he could be reached by his step-son's emissaries and come to the latter's aid if need be.[19] Sir William Stanley need not have been so circumspect in his manoeuvres; he had declared himself for Henry, was determined to avenge himself on King Richard, and had openly collaborated with the rebels from Shrewsbury onwards. His public denouncement as a traitor five days or so before had sealed his fate one way or another.[20]

The formation that the Stanleys were attempting to contrive is supported by the ballad tradition – that Lord Thomas Stanley took the 'vanward' and his brother, Sir William Stanley, the 'rereward'.[21] In other words, Lord Stanley advanced first, in order that he might be seen still to give the appearance of joining Richard's formations. At Henry's request, he allowed a contingent from his own army, headed by four knights – Sir Robert Tunstall, Sir John Savage, Sir Hugh Pearsall and Sir Humphrey Stanley – to comprise a professional striking unit in Henry's vanguard, whilst he himself remained in his intermediate position on a hill midway between the two armies but in the sight of both.[22] Sir William Stanley, following behind (the 'rereward'), is shown in the ballads to be in communication with his brother (and must therefore have been on the same side of the battle) though ostensibly separated. It may be, therefore, that Lord Stanley's forces were ranged on the brow of the hillside at Dadlington, whilst Sir William Stanley's forces were behind the brow of the hill at Stoke Golding.[23] It was important for neither of the Stanleys to reveal too much of his presence or tactics to Richard's eyes on Ambion Hill.

It is clear from the more reliable of the sources that Lord Stanley kept to his tactics of remaining physically uncommitted, although this seems to be denied by certain of the foreign accounts. Jean Molinet, for example, records that 'le seigneur de Scandelay' came in good time to the aid of Earl Henry and helped destroy Richard's vanguard.[24] Another foreign source, the Spaniard de Valera, records that the 'Lord Tamorlant' (if we read for Tamorlant, Stanley) formed part of Richard's left wing and, moving in front of the king's vanguard, turned around to attack it.[25] Apart from the doubtful mechanics of such a manoeuvre, we have to bear in mind, in the first place, that these two foreign sources are less reliable *vis à vis* the tactics of the peripheral forces in the battle, and in the second place, that neither takes account of the separate force of Sir William Stanley, to a large extent dependent on his brother's orders.

Moreover, both Molinet and de Valera can to some extent be reconciled, in that it was indeed Sir William Stanley who came to the aid of Henry, and furthermore, that contingents from Lord Stanley's force were indeed deputed to Henry's vanguard at the beginning of the battle. Furthermore, as we have already seen, it was important that Lord Stanley be seen to be technically part of Richard's forces – indeed as a kind of vanguard (as noted by Pittscottie):[26] and by virtue of the fact that de Valera distinguishes him as being on the left wing, we are given a clear indication that Thomas Stanley was to the south of the battlefield on the line of hills across the valley of the Sence brook.

We now come to the question of Henry's own tactics. Again, Polydore Vergil's text has been misread in some crucial respects. Ross, for example, claimed that the description Vergil gives of Oxford's van flanked by Sir John Savage and Sir Gilbert Talbot is an unlikely formation in fifteenth century warfare.[27] The customary practice, he argues, was to have a vanguard comprising archers and footmen, and then a strong body of knights and professional *milites* positioned behind in the 'main battel'.

This description of fifteenth century battle-formations, however, coincides exactly with that really given in Vergil, for Vergil does not describe a vanguard (*prima acies*) as such at this point but only a battle-line (*acies*).[28] Thus, Vergil describes Henry placing his archers in front of the battle-line, commanded by the Earl of Oxford, and then the wings (*cornus*) of the battle-line on the left and right, commanded respectively by Sir John Savage and Sir Gilbert Talbot.[29] The entire 'battel' effectively comprised the vanguard which, in this instance and by virtue of Henry's small numbers (and also because he was relying upon reinforcements from his step-father), constituted the principal force of arms. This pattern was repeated at the later battles of East Stoke (1487) and Black-heath (1497), where Henry committed his vanguards alone to the fray, and personally remained, in the latter case at least, as though aloof from the battle.[30]

Vergil's distinction between 'battle line' and 'vanguard' has been noted by Bennett.[31] So too should Vergil's use of the word *procul*, for this may also be crucial in our interpretation of the complex manoeuvres of the battle, as in the passage following his description of Henry's formations:

> So each of the battle-lines being arrayed, when the armies were able to
> see each other afar off, they put on their helmets and prepared to fight.[32]

A recent translation of this line suggests that the armies were on the move before they came in sight of each other, whereas Vergil's syntax implies that they contrived their formations and moved when mutual visibility was assured.[33] This translation has been used to support the contention that Henry's army travelled a distance of several miles to the site of the battle (presumably in formation). However, this is not only unlikely in practice, but does not accord with sources such as Jean Molinet, who specifically states that the preparations for battle were made when the armies were a quarter of a league from one another (that is, approximately three-quarters of a mile).[34]

There follows in Vergil's account a description of the marsh (*palus*). Vergil relates that a marsh lay between the two armies, which Henry used as a defence on his right-hand side, and in so doing put the sun at his back.[35] This manoeuvre is said to be done *de industria* – that is, tactically. There is nothing here about the sun shining in the faces of Henry's enemies, nor, as Williams has it, about the marsh being a defence to King Richard's army.[36] It is clear, however, that Henry needed to gain the advantage of the ground, since the king appeared to have the best defensive position and the advantage of the sun. As Henry was a relative novice in military strategy, this was no doubt the advice given by professional commanders. Amongst these were his uncle, Jasper Earl of Pembroke, and the Earl of Oxford himself who, leading the vanguard, was the first to engage the king's forces. Both Jean Molinet and *The Rose of Englande* ballad describe an attack on the flank of Richard's army (*de costé à la bataille* in Molinet).[37] An important stanza in *The Rose of Englande* specifies that this was accomplished by Oxford's vanguard and to the north of the south-west/north-east diagonal axis, since it was aimed at the right wing of Richard's van:

> then the blew bore [Oxford] the vanguard had:
> he was both warry and wise of witt;
> the right hand of them he took,
> the sunn and wind of them to gett.[38]

Molinet's account suggests that the rebels' wheeling action was to avoid the king's gunfire, but it was also a response to the 'situation of the place and the order of his battle'.[39] Certainly, it was an intelligent tactic in the light of the conditions that prevailed. In a single manoeuvre Oxford was able to get a south-westerly (prevailing) wind on his side for his archers, to avoid direct sunlight from the south-east, to use the marsh as a protection on his right and to pick off the northerly arm (*cornus*) of a cumbersome vanguard already drawn up by the king, and commanded by the Duke of Norfolk. Oxford was using classic military strategy as laid down in Vegetius' *De Re Militari*.[40]

Having concentrated on Henry's tactics we turn now to the disposition of King Richard's army. The word Vergil uses when his narrative changes scene is *interea*, meanwhile. The word *interea*, therefore, often implies re-tracing the time sequence in order to describe parallel actions. Vergil's diction and syntax are coherent in a quite precise way: the narrative deals first with Henry's moves up to his secret meeting with the Stanleys near Atherstone, then with Richard's advance to Ambion and the ordering of his vanguard, and next with Henry's encampment near the battlefield and the preparations for the encounter. It seems probable that, on the morning of the battle, the king was the less prepared of the two. The confusion in King Richard's camp at dawn, when the chaplains were not ready to celebrate mass and no breakfast was prepared, was psychologically hardly conducive to the good conduct of an impending battle.[41] In addition, several of the sources suggest that Henry's formations were advancing before the king was fully prepared.[42]

The *Crowland Chronicle* states that the king had marched out of Leicester in great pomp, wearing the crown on his head, and accompanied by John Howard Duke of Norfolk, and Henry Percy Earl of Northumberland.[43] The order of Richard's march from Nottingham to Leicester the previous day (20th August) was probably repeated: that is, the baggage and armaments travelled in a central train, followed directly by the king and his entourage. Presumably, Norfolk's army went ahead, with Northumberland's making up the rear.[44] This would coincide with likely dispositions at the battlefield itself, where Norfolk commanded the vanguard, and Northumberland – to use Drayton's phrase – a full 'three quarters of a mile' behind the lines.[45]

The road the king took is not known for sure, although strong local tradition does describe him leaving Leicester by the west gate, across the water-meadows adjacent to the Augustinian Priory, and thus towards Leicester Forest.[46] It is usually assumed that he took the route of the Roman road (to Mancetter), but it is doubtful whether the eastern sector of this road still existed in the fifteenth century.[47] Perhaps a more likely way was through the relatively open chase of Leicester Forest towards Earl Shilton. At the western gate of the forest, below the hill on which Earl Shilton stands, the king would have faced a choice of routes. His 'scurryers' having informed him that Henry's army was at Atherstone, he would have had no need to continue south-westward to the Watling Street to cut off Henry's route to London, but rather to seek battle nearer Atherstone. Accordingly, he needed to turn due westward. A possible passage, hitherto unknown, might be conjectured. At the base of Shilton hill an ancient track, possibly an old Salt Way, seems to have crossed the country from east to west. This may pre-date the Roman road-system, and there is some indication that parts of it remained in use as a green road up to the eighteenth century.[48] This route westward crossed the summit of Ambion Hill and might therefore have been the road used by the king to reach his advantageous camp-site. At any rate, the evidence for Ambion as the site of Richard's camp is substantial, and it accounts for the tradition by which a spring on the hill is named after the king.[49]

In considering King Richard's tactics on the morning of the battle, we have to dispense once and for all with the notion that the battle of Bosworth involved the defence of a hill against an assault on it by an ostensibly smaller army. This is Hutton's view followed by Kendall, Ross and Williams.[50] The idea is not only implausible but unsubstantiated by any evidence. As we have already established, the battle was fought on a plain – the plain of Redemore. Thus, Richard's purpose was to get his army into position on the plain in order to encounter an enemy already in an advanced state of preparation. In doing this, he seems first to have consolidated his main 'battle', as Henry had done, into the vanguard, with a front line of archers led by the Duke of Norfolk. Vergil shows this to have been a long and formidable battle-line intended to put fear into the hearts of the enemy.[51] An elevated position above the plain – such as the 300 foot contour line of Ambion – would have reinforced this intention, although the small hillock on which stands the present Apple Orchard Farm (at approx. 295 feet) also constitutes an elevated platform, and might therefore have been a convenient point of departure for the advance of the king's army.

The sequence of events that follows is unclear, and a coherent description of what happened remains elusive. However, some patterns do emerge if we bear in mind the probability, as Goodman has suggested, that two areas of fighting opened up half a mile or so distant from each other.[52]

The battle between the vanguards, on which both commanders had staked so much, clearly took place in an area north of the south-west/north-east diagonal axis (see fig.3). This is evidenced by *The Rose of Englande* ballad and is also suggested by the positioning of the Duke of Norfolk on the wing *(ala)* of Richard's vanguard, as described by the Crowland Chronicler.[53] It may be that Norfolk, the chief commander of Richard's van, although ostensibly leading the archers, was forced to position himself to one side (thus, on the wing) by reason of Oxford's manoeuvre or even indeed because of the nature of the terrain. Obviously this would have been a move to the right (the north) if Norfolk faced Oxford. Such a position is further supported by a detail in *Ladye Bessiye* that it was Sir John Savage (on the left of Oxford's vanguard) who finally cornered the Duke of Norfolk in the vicinity of a windmill.[54]

The tactical superiority of King Richard's imposing battle line also had its drawbacks. The over-extended array, although superficially awesome, was unwieldy in military terms and, in the event, was broken up. The *Bosworth Feilde* ballad and Polydore Vergil corroborate each other here. Having forced

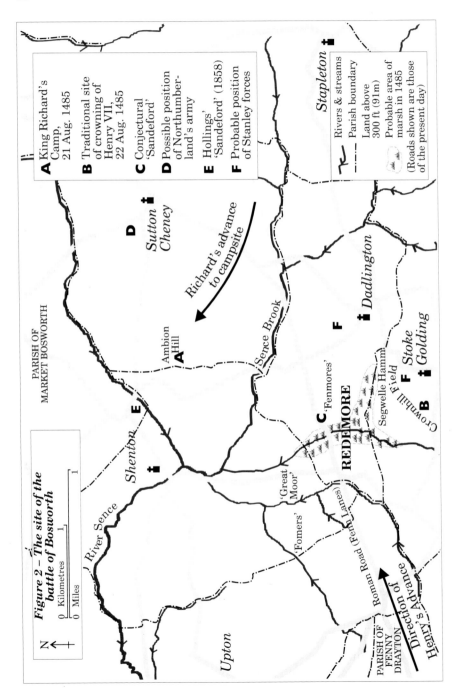

Figure 2 – The site of the battle of Bosworth

Richard's battle line to concentrate itself in its northern wing, Oxford made sure that his own men were tightly-packed so that they could not be broken by superior numbers.[55] Vergil's text, read correctly, details the brilliance of the manoeuvre. It was not Oxford's formation that was 'in array tryangle' (as the awkward sixteenth century translation has it),[56] but the forces of the other contingents of the vanguard; that is, presumably, those commanded by Savage and Talbot among others. According to *Ladye Bessiye* it was Rhys ap Thomas's men who broke the king's battle-line.[57] This would suggest that Rhys was one of the commanders in the vanguard, and may be included under Vergil's general phrase *et alii in parte altera* (and the others in the other part).[58] The specific formation which is described by Vergil was a classic of military strategy from Roman times onwards: a compact column of men *(cuneus)* penetrate a slender line at right-angles, separating soldiers from their commanders and enabling a fragmented force to be tackled piece-meal. This coincides with the ballad account in which one of the king's men warned him about the danger of delaying action further as a result of being distracted by the execution of Lord Strange: 'Our ray breaketh on every side; we put our ffolke in jeopardye'.[59] It was due to the failure of Lord Stanley to assist and reinforce the king at this point that Richard became diverted by the need to make an example of Stanley's son; but then his failure to carry the command through may also have been an ominous lapse of authority at a crucial juncture.[60]

King Richard's next move was desperate but necessary. Recognising treachery on several fronts – certainly by Thomas Stanley and possibly by Northumberland who, according to the Crowland Chronicler, was 'stationed in a part of the field where no encounter was discernible and no battle-blows given or received'[61] – the king decided to bring matters to a crisis. The vanguard was already in difficulty and to reinforce it himself would have been to abandon a part of the field where danger may have erupted as a result of the treachery of the Stanleys.[62] The only possibility of success was to attack and destroy the enemy's chief commander, the Earl of Richmond himself. Vergil appears to describe moves made by the king to ascertain more clearly the banner of Henry's bodyguard.[63] When this was assured, according to Vergil, the king 'charged at him out of the other side beyond the battle line'.[64] Vergil's phrase is crucial because it indicates the direction of Richard's charge, that is, to the south of the axis. His words *ex altero latere* (out of the other side) imply a direction on the opposite side of the battle to the one he has just described in his text – that is, the battle of the vanguard, which we have already established was to the north. We therefore have a situation in which Richard descended from his hill in a south-westerly direction with a small army of select knights, recognised Henry situated *procul* (far off) with a small bodyguard, and sought to end the battle by a personal assault.[65] Both Jean

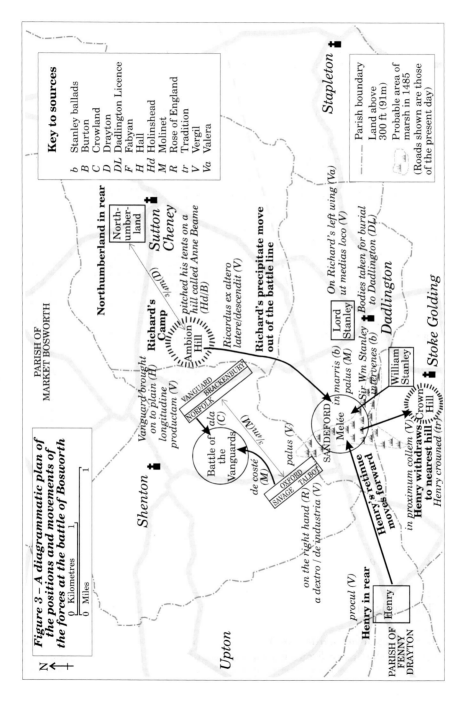

Figure 3 – A diagrammatic plan of the positions and movements of the forces at the battle of Bosworth

Molinet and the Harley 542 manuscript suggest that the final stages of the battle occurred in the vicinity of a marsh – presumably the same marsh or area of wetland shown by Vergil to have lain between the two armies at the start of the battle and which Oxford's formation had avoided by veering north.

Harley 542 omits the process by which Richard found himself in the wetland, since this event is bracketed both with the intervention of Sir William Stanley and then with Richard's death. The final *melée* in which Richard's household knights were attacked by Sir William Stanley coming 'downe at a banke', must therefore correspond very closely with the situation in which King Richard and his men are described as being 'in a marris'.[66] If we are to believe de Valera, it was the Spanish mercenary 'le Petit Salazar' who encouraged the king to escape because of the treason of his followers.[67] According to both Vergil and the *Bosworth Feilde* tradition, Richard refused to flee when a horse was made ready for him.[68] The contraction of the time-sequence in these sources presents problems, but the offer of a horse would seem to coincide with the realisation that the battle line was broken and treachery was manifest. It was subsequent to this that the king descended into the fray, wearing his crown, and wielding his battle-axe.[69] According to Molinet, it was a Welshman who dealt the final blow with a halbert, when Richard's horse stumbled in the marsh *(palus)*. This detail is endorsed, perhaps predictably, in Welsh tradition.[70]

The death of a chief commander in fifteenth century warfare invariably signalled the end of the battle.[71] Vergil describes the remaining soldiers laying down their weapons or fleeing. Many seemed to have walked away from the battle unharmed, since there is no mention of captives among the ordinary soldiery.[72] The battle of the vanguards, however, was attended by a rout *(fuga)* in which, according to Vergil, many were slain, but whose direction is not given.[73] A plausible assumption would be that it was to the east or north-east, but at any rate in the area where the battle of the vanguards was fought, and presumably away from the enemy. The death of the king and therefore the end of the battle are likely to have occurred to the south of the axis, in all probability in Dadlington chapelry, which afterwards received a licence to assist the establishment of a battlefield chantry. Vergil tells us that Henry then withdrew *in proximum collem* – 'to the nearest (or adjacent) hill', where he gave thanks to God, ordered that the wounded and dead should be attended to, and received the royal crown 'found among the spoils of the field'.[74]

The battlefield 'crowning' of Henry Tudor also presents problems, due to a divergence of opinion amongst the primary sources as to whether it was Lord Thomas or Sir William Stanley who was responsible for this. It has been pointed out that Lord Stanley swore an oath before a papal commission on 16 January 1486 that he had not known his step-son until two days after the battle of Bosworth,[75] which, if credible, might indicate that Stanley's caution before the battle was such that he could not be seen to be personally involved in negotiations with his step-son, and, further, that he was not involved in the battlefield 'crowning'. It might be argued, therefore, that Vergil's account was distorted by the fall from favour and execution of Sir William Stanley in 1495, it being impolitic to record in an official history that Henry VII was honoured by a man twice declared traitor. In contrast, the *Great Chronicle of London*, though at second hand, describes Sir William Stanley presenting the crown to Henry in an act which implies unprecedented spontaneity ('Incontynently, as It was said').[76] This may have a ring of truth in that Sir William was closely involved with the death of the king, and news of this kind is more likely to have filtered through to London and to be accurately reflected in a contemporary annal than is the case in the more partisan source of the Stanley ballad tradition or in the more judicious latter-day account of Polydore Vergil.

The battlefield 'crowning' traditionally took place on the western spur of the hill on which the village of Stoke Golding stands, called Crown Hill. This site alone had been identified as the spot long before William Hutton, and so reinforces the probability that the battle of Bosworth ended in the vicinity of Stoke Golding and in the chapelry of Dadlington, which extends westward a short distance from Crown Hill. The name Crown Hill can be traced in records as far back as 1605, when the Harrington estate at Stoke was sold to its tenant farmers. A deed of sale describes closes called 'Crown hill' and 'Hollow meadow' severalled from 'Crownehill field', which seems to have been (in c.1600) the name of the open field in the north-western quarter of Stoke Golding.[77] Nichols, in 1782, reported skeletal remains often dug up in Crown-hill field, when gravel was extracted for road repairs.[78] It is likely that in this area too the finds of weaponry and arrow-heads described by Burton (1622) were located, at a time when the fields were being allotted to their new owners.

King Richard's body, covered in 'mud and filth', was taken from the place where it fell – possibly a ford across an arm of the wetland in the valley below Dadlington – and, stripped bare, was carried across the back of a horse to Leicester, where it was displayed for two days in the church of St. Mary of the Annunciation in the Newarke, and afterwards buried unceremoniously at the Grey Friars monastery near St. Martin's church.[79] Ten years later, an alabaster monument was erected over the grave, one Walter Hylton of Nottingham being commissioned to sculpt it. The fate of that tomb is another story, and beyond the scope of the present study, but it does seem likely that the remains of the last Plantagenet king of England still lie buried in an unknown place in the vicinity of the street called Grey Friars in the heart of Leicester.[80]

NOTES

Chapter One

1. L. Campbell, *Shakespeare's 'Histories'* (San Marino, California: Huntingdon Library, 1947). Richard Grafton's continuation of John Hardyng's *Chronicle* came out in 1543. He utilised material from Polydore Vergil, with additions from More in his treatment of Richard III's reign. See R. Grafton, *History of the Reigns of Edward IV, Edward V, and Richard III*, ed. H. Ellis (London, 1812).

2. W. Shakespeare, *King Richard the Third*, Act IV. sc. v., l.1, in *William Shakespeare: The Complete Works*, ed. Peter Alexander (London, 1951),740 (hereafter, Shakespeare). Urswick's role in the days before the battle of Bosworth is described in Polydore Vergil's MS of the *Anglica Historia* (1534), but omitted from the printed versions. See D. Hay, *Polydore Vergil: Renaissance Historian and Man of Letters* (Oxford, 1952), 207. Hay gives the omitted passage concerning Urswick's mission to rally support for Richmond. Christopher Urswick was a friend of Vergil's and gave him *viva voce* information about the battle after 1502.

3. Shakespeare, 742 (Act V, sc. iii, l.37). This positioning coincides with a clue in the Spanish councillor's letter, an independent near-contemporary report of the battle of Bosworth. (See Chap. 4, n.25).

4. Shakespeare, 744, 746 (Act V, sc. iii, l.177; Act V, sc. iv, ll.7, 13). Again, the loss of the king's horse is not found in the standard histories, although it is supported by the independent evidence of the near-contemporary *Chronicle* of Jean Molinet, a Burgundian commentator. It may have been a potent local (and oral) tradition, as is partly indicated by the story of Jane Dixie's testimony recorded in J. Nichols, *The History and Antiquities of Leicestershire*, IV, (London, 1811), 554. Jane Dixie was a spinster niece of Sir Wolstan Dixie, 3rd Baronet of Bosworth Park, and died at Newbold Verdon in 1779. She is reported to have read some old manuscripts found in Sutton Hall in the eighteenth century, and certainly her reminiscences of their contents are not so easily reconciled with the kind of information that would have been otherwise available to her, whilst some of the details are corroborated by other evidence. This point is taken up by Michael Bennett in his *The Battle of Bosworth* (Gloucester, 1985), 10. (hereafter, Bennett).

5. R. Holinshed, *Chronicles of England, Scotlande, and Irelande...* (London, 1577), 1417 ff. (hereafter, Holinshed); E.Hall, *The Union of the Two Noble and Illustre Families of Lancastre and Yorke* [1548], 'The Tragicall Doynges of Kynge Richard the Thirde' (London, 1550), f.xxx ff. (hereafter, Hall).

6. Although Vergil uses paraphrases of speeches on occasion. The *Crowland Chronicle* reports that King Richard did 'affirm' and 'express' his view of the cause and his intentions in the pending battle, but leaves it unclear as to whether this information was for the consumption of his commanders or his men. The bleak content of his message might seem to favour the former.

7. Hall's phrase in Henry's 'oration' that 'before us be our enemies, and on ether side of us be such as I neither surely trust, nor greatly beleve' has been used to support the contention that this refers to the Stanley forces ranged on either side of the battlefield; but as Bennett points out, it could equally mean Northumberland's army as well as the Stanleys. See Bennett, 107.

8. 'Historia Croylandensis Continuatio', in W.Fulman (ed.), *Rerum Anglicanum Scriptorum* (London, 1684), 574. (hereafter, *Crowland Chronicle*).

9. Ibid., 574. Translations of the *Crowland Chronicle* are found in Bennett, 157, and in N. Pronay and J.Cox, *The Crowland Chronicle Continuations 1459-1486* (Richard III and Yorkist History Trust, 1986). H. T. Riley's original translation of the second continuation appears in *Ingulph's Chronicles* (London: Bohn Antiquarian Library, 1893), 501-5.

10. The phrase Vergil uses when he is reporting spurious tradition or hearsay; see D. Hay, op. cit., 92.

11. *Crowland Chronicle*, 594. It has been pointed out that the phrase used by the anonymous continuator specifically indicates that divine service was not *prepared* rather than that (as Riley's translation suggests) chaplains were not present. This has led to the unwarranted assumption that the chaplains were left behind in Leicester (see D.T. Williams, '"A Place Mete for Twoo Battayles to Encountre": the Siting of the Battle of Bosworth, 1485', *The Ricardian* VII, no.90 (September, 1985), 89.). This provides a good example

of how ambiguous translations can mislead. see M.J. Phillips, 'The Battle of Bosworth: Further Reflections on the Battlefield Site', *The Ricardian* VII, no.96 (January, 1987), 361-2.

12. The date and authorship of the *Crowland Chronicle* have been exhaustively discussed in recent years, and there is still no consensus of opinion on this. However, it is an important primary source for contemporary events, although the anonymous author may well have been in retirement and away from the scene of action at the time of the battle. Alison Hanham's view is that the second continuation shows evidence of having been compiled by a clerical redactor interpolating in an *ur*-text by a royal councillor. Pronay and Cox argue at some length for the single authorship of the work during ten days at Crowland Abbey, finishing on 30 April 1486. They suggest Henry Sharp, Doctor of 'Civil Law' as author. For the various arguments, see A. Hanham, *Richard III and His Early Historians* (Oxford, 1975); J.G. Edwards, 'The "Second" Continuation of the Crowland Chronicle; Was it Written "in Ten Days"?', *Bulletin of the Institute of Historical Research* XXXIX, no.100 (November 1966); N. Pronay and J. Cox, op. cit.; H.A. Kelly, 'The Croyland Chronicle Tragedies', *The Ricardian* VII, no.99 (December 1987); and, as a note on the problems of translating the Crowland Chronicle *vis à vis* Pronay and Cox's version, see also L. Visser-Fuchs, 'A Commentary on the Continuation', *The Ricardian* VII, no.99 (December 1987).

13. B.L.Add.MS 12060 ff. 19-20. Mentioned in *Forty-Six Lives Translated from Boccaccio's "De Claris Mulieribus" by Henry Parker, Lord Morley*, ed. H.G. Wright (Early English Text Society, first ser., 214, 1943 for 1940). Lord Morley was the son of Sir William Parker (d.1510), who was standard-bearer and counsellor to Richard III. See also R. Warnicke, 'Sir Ralph Bigod: A Loyal Servant to King Richard III', *The Ricardian* VI, No 84 (March 1984), 299-303

14. Hall, f.xxxiiii.

15. *Sustinuit tamen Henricus impetum diutius, quam etiam eius milites putarant.* Polydore Vergil, *Anglica Historia* (Basle, 1534), 556 (hereafter, Polydore Vergil).

16. *Et quia omnis spes salutis in armis erat, se certamini avide offert.* Polydore Vergil, 556.

17. Henry VII established squires of the body to act as a personal retinue. Robert Harcourt, dispossessed by Richard III of his father's estates at Market Bosworth, fought for Henry VII in 1485, and was created squire of the body for his services. See P.J. Foss, *The History of Market Bosworth* (Wymondham, 1983), 18-19.

18. Hall, f.xxxiii; Polydore Vergil, 556.

19. Ibid. The Tudor translation does not distinguish between 'battle-line' and 'vanguard' in Vergil, but translates *acies* in this instance as 'vanward'. This could lead to confusion about the position of the king in relation to his forces.

20. See below. The Stanley ballads consolidated in song a common oral record of the events of the battle, possibly originating in eye- witness reports. Our earliest manuscript survival of this tradition is the Stow MS Harley 542, f.31-3, first printed by J. Nichols in *The History and Antiquities of the County of Leicester* IV, pt.ii (London, 1811), (hereafter, Nichols). The traditions contained in these ballads were known in Shakespeare's day, since manuscript versions of the Ladye Bessiye ballad date from c.1600.

21. M. Drayton, *Poly-Olbion*, song XXII (1622) in J. William Hebel (ed.), *The Works of Michael Drayton* (Oxford, 1961), IV, 460.

22. Sir George Buck, *The History of Richard III* (1619), ed. A. Noel Kincaid (Gloucester, 1979), 99.

23. W.Burton, *The Description of Leicestershire* (London, 1622), 47. (hereafter, Burton).

24. 'Kyng Richard, beynge furnished with men & all abilimentes of war, bringyng all his men out of there camp into ye plaine'. Hall, f.xxx.

25. C.L. Kingsford, *English Historical Literature in the Fifteenth Century* (Oxford, 1913), (hereafter, Kingsford). See also C.L. Kingsford (ed.), *Chronicles of London* (Oxford, 1905).

26. Kingsford, 101.

27. Kingsford, 74.

28. The *Great Chronicle* is preserved in the Guildhall Library MS 3313. See A.H. Thomas and I.D. Thornley (eds.), *The Great Chronicle of London* (London, 1938), 237. (hereafter, the *Great Chronicle*).

29. Kingsford, 101, 105-6. I take *Fabyan's Chronicle* as a later work than the *Great Chronicle* and influenced by it, though the traditional view is that Fabyan wrote both. Stylistic differences throw doubt on this. See J.M.W. Bean, 'The Role of Robert Fabyan in Tudor Historiography of the "Wars of the Roses"', in Karl-Ludwig Selig and Robert Somerville (eds.), *Florilegium Columbianum: Essays in Honor of Paul Oskar Kristeller* (New York: Italica Press, 1987).

30. Robert Fabyan, *Chronicle* (London, 1516), 'Septima Pars Richardi tertii', f.ccxxx. (hereafter, Fabyan).

31. There were two further editions - of 1546 and 1555 - both of them revised by Polydore Vergil himself, although the major revisions took place between the MS of c.1513 and the first edition of 1534. It is important to note therefore the meticulous way in which Vergil monitored the progress of his book. Vergil was an Italian clerk, born c. 1480, who came to England in 1502 and received royal patronage at the Tudor court. He died in Urbino in 1559.

32. See D.Hay, *Polydore Vergil: Renaissance Historian and Man of Letters* (Oxford, 1952), 79-80 (hereafter, Hay). See also D. Hay, 'The Manuscript of Polydore Vergil's *"Anglica Historia"*,' *Eng. Hist. Rev.* LIV (1939), 241-3. The MS, now in the Vatican Library, was first discovered by F. Gasquet - see *Trans. Royal Hist. Soc.*,n.s. XVI (1902). In the MS Vergil wrote:

> "When on approaching our own times, I could find no such annals.... I betook myself to every man of age who was pointed out to me as having been formerly occupied in important and public affairs, and from all such I obtained information about events up to the year 1500. From that time - since I came to England immediately after that date - I have myself noted down, day by day, everything of importance."

33. Fabyan reflects popular myth, beginning his *Chronicle* with the Creation, and the foundation of Britain by Brutus. See Hay, 147.

34. Hay, 109. Vergil's ostensible refusal to acknowledge the Dissolution of the Monasteries in all three printed versions of the *Anglica Historia* is a strange case in point, noted by Hay.

35. Classical standards for sixteenth century historians were laid down in Cicero's *De Oratione* II. See Hay, 151-4.

36. Polydore Vergil, 554-5.

37. *ultra acies*. Polydore Vergil, 556.

38. *Ricardus inter confertissimos hostes praelians interficitur*. Ibid, 557.

39. *in certamen descendit, ut aut initium, finemue regnandi ex illo faceret*. Ibid, 557. Hay, 94, suggests this oral source was considered by Vergil to be reliable.

40. Hay, 164 ff., discusses the language used by Vergil's translators and borrowers. Note also the divergence of meaning of the word 'field' in Edward Hall, as shown in the definition given in the O.E.D. (1901), IV, i, 192.86. This is discussed below.

41. BL MS Royal, C. ix; published by H. Ellis (ed.), in *Three Books of Polydore Vergil's English History,* Camden Society XXIX (1844). This translation is from the 1546 edition, and goes only up to 1485.

42. J. Stow, *The Annales of England...* (London, 1592),781-3.The denigration of Polydore in the sixteenth century began with Leland's defence of Geoffrey of Monmouth whom Vergil derided. This developed into a 'fantastic process of defamation' from Elizabethan times onwards, and was still current in the early part of the twentieth century, despite no evidence in support of the charges of bias and corruption of sources levelled at Vergil. See Hay, 155.

43. J. Speed, *The History of Great Britaine...* (London, 1611). (hereafter, Speed). F. Baker, *Chronicle* (London, 1643); F. Sandford, *A Genealogical History of the Kings and Queens of England* (London, 1677).

44. Speed, 725. Stow, op.cit., 782, has 'out of the side of the range of his battaile'.

45. Speed, 725.

46. See above, note 39.

47. Speed, 725. Speed also includes information about what happened to the king's body after its return to Leicester, its burial at Greyfriars, the tomb erected over it by King Henry, and its subsequent

desecration. The reliability of this information is discussed in C.J. Billson, *Medieval Leicester* (Leicester, 1920), 180-6.

48. Speed, 723. Ambion Hill is eleven-and-a-half statute miles west of Leicester.

49. Holinshed, 1416. It might be worth remembering that Holinshed's *Chronicle* was a compilation by a syndicate, among whom William Harrison provided the descriptive matter about England and Richard Hooker, the history. It seems very likely that one of them had access to oral information about the locality: hence the interpolations concerning Ambion and the progress of draining in the adjacent marshland.

50. Hall, f.xxx.

51. J.Speed, *The Atlas and Theatre of Great Britaine* (London, 1611).

52. R.K.Baum, *Antique Maps of Leicestershire* (Loughborough, 1981), 45. The anonymous 'Smith' map of 1602 was a correction and augmentation of Saxton's in which Burton had a hand (vide, Preface, *The Description of Leicestershire*). However, it was the amended Kip map, first used in Camden's *Britannica* that Burton adopted as a frontispiece in his own book. That the spelling 'Redmore' was not strictly a *corruption* but rather an alternative form, probably adopted in the south-east of England only at an early date, is shown by the 15th century Frowick Chronicle (see A.F. Sutton and L. Visser-Fuchs, 'The Making of a Minor London Chronicle in the Household of Sir Thomas Frowick (Died 1485)', *The Ricardian* X, No. 126 (Sept. 1994)). It was the interpretation of a misunderstood etymology that led to corruptions of meaning.

53. B.L.Harley 542, ff.31-3v. It is headed 'borowyd of Henry Savyll'. Henry Savile the elder of Blaithroyd 'alias the Banke' (d. 1607) corresponded with Stow in the 1570s. The Saviles were an important landholding family in Halifax in the 1580s and 90s.

54. J.W. Hales and F.J. Furnivall (eds.)., *Bishop Percy's Folio Manuscript: Ballads and Romances* (London, 1868), III, 233ff. Bishop Percy's MS is in B.L. Add. MS 27879. (hereafter, Hales and Furnivall).

55. C. Ross, *Richard III* (London 1981), Appendix II, 235.

56. *Ladye Bessiye* is also printed in Hales and Furnivall, 391 ff. in its later version. The earlier one (B.L. Harley MS 367, f.89 ff.) was printed by the Percy Society, XX, (London, 1847), 38 ff.

57. The ballads are discussed by Joan Williams in 'The Stanley Family of Lathom and Knowsley 1450-1504. A Political Study', M.A. Thesis, University of Manchester 1979. She distinguishes between a Yorkshire and a Lancastrian tradition represented respectively by *Bosworth Feilde* and *Ladye Bessiye*.

Chapter Two

1. S. Piggott, 'Antiquarian Thought in the Sixteenth and Seventeenth Centuries', in *Ruins in a Landscape: Essays in Antiquarianism* (Edinburgh, 1976), 21, 49.

2. Ibid., 52.

3. H. Walpole, *Historic Doubts on the Life and Reign of King Richard the Third* (1768), (Wakefield, Yorkshire, 1974).

4. D.T. Williams, 'William Hutton and the Eighteenth Century Rediscovery of Bosworth Field', *The Leicestershire Historian* III, no.3 (1984/5), 6.

5. Catherine Hutton, *The Life of William Hutton* (London, 1817), 184.

6. P.J. Foss, *The History of Market Bosworth* (Wymondham, 1983), 99-100.

7. J. Throsby, *Select Views in Leicestershire* (Leicester, 1789), I, 338.

8. W. Hutton, *The Battle of Bosworth-Field* (1788), (Birmingham, 1813), 8. (hereafter, Hutton). I am quoting from Nichols' second edition of the work, since it contains Hutton's letters in response to Nichols' enquiries. Apart from these the material remains unaltered from the first edition.

9. Hutton, Preface, vii.

10. Ibid., Preface, vii, 8.

11. Ibid., Preface, vii.

12. Ibid., Preface, viii.

13. Ibid.

14. Ibid., 94.

15. Ibid., 49-50, 62-3. The tradition of King Richard's officers sleeping in the village church at Elmesthorpe seems to have originated with Hutton. The Bradshaws is a nineteenth century farmhouse half a mile south of Stapleton village. The supposed 'breast work' mentioned by Hutton has been identified with a possible field boundary at SP 430980. Since Pridden's map of 1789, the Ordnance Survey from the First Series 1835 map onwards, has marked King Richard's encampment here; the Survey's adoption of the Pridden map information extended to adopting its faults, such as the erroneous placing of Ambion Hill in Stapleton instead of in Sutton. Gamble's Close, Hutton's position for Lord Stanley's camp, corresponds with the farmhouse called Hopewell on the 1835 O.S. map, and is synonymous with the close called 'Owpale' in early seventeenth century title-deeds in Stoke Golding parish (although the connection with 'Gamble' is not evident). Aerial archaeology has shown no evidence of earthworks or crop marks here, and there is no tradition of such (J.Pickering F.S.A.: pers. comm.). A southern position for the Stanley camp is, however, likely (see below). As for the Whitemoors, we cannot find this name mentioned in any documents belonging to Shenton from the seventeenth century onwards, and consequently this may be a non-indigenous name deriving from Hutton. However, the name is a common micro-tponym, and as Barrie Cox has pointed out, may have emerged later at a local level to describe 'dry' land (from A.S. 'wite' = 'dry'), in contradistinction to former wet land. Again, the O.S. maps since 1835, following Hutton's identifications, have tended to place Richmond's camp here; however, it is somewhat uncertain whether Hutton's description on p.66 corresponds exactly with the positioning on later ordnance survey maps. The 1854 Tithe Map of Shenton gives a 'Camp Close' at SP 385988, but this is a late enclosure, and the nomenclature is not found on earlier estate maps.

16. See Hutton's map. There are other curious numerical symbolisms; see p.135-6.

17. Hutton, 95.

18. Ibid., 108. This idea of an assault on a hill, with an attack up an ascent against a superior force, which derives from Hutton but which cannot be discovered in any source for the battle, has been so influential as to form the basis of descriptions in Kendall, Ross, Williams et al. See C. Ross, *Richard III* (London, 1981), 220.

19. Hutton, 107.

20. Ibid., 128. The hollows which Hutton identified were in all likelihood 'fen holes' such as are mentioned in sixteenth century records relating to land in Stoke Golding parish (see below). Hutton refers to Burton's account of battle accoutrements being found in this area, although Burton makes no mention of human bones, which Hutton's account suggests.

21. Hutton, 127, 132-3. 'Hollow Meadow' was probably named after the fen holes referred to above. It first appears in early seventeenth century documents. The thornbush legend is curious. Hutton seems to be the inventor of details about the soldier and possibly of Sir Reginald Bray. The device of a crown in a bush in Westminster Abbey would seem to refer to a rosebush, although something like a thornbush does appear in Tudor iconography of the sixteenth century. However, nowhere is this specifically related to this legend, the earliest mention of which we can find being F. Sandford, *A Genealogical History of England* (London, 1677). See also, P. Tudor-Craig, *Richard III Catalogue,* (London, 1973), 17, and C. Ross, *The Wars of the Roses* (London, 1976), 12-13. My thanks to Mr. Michael Archer of the Victoria and Albert Museum, and to Dr. Hilary Wayment of Cambridge for their help in this regard.

22. Hall, f.xxx.

23. Holinshed, 1416.

24. In Staffordshire Record Office, D 649/4/1.

25. In the late fifteenth century 'field' could indicate both the place of battle and also the encounter itself. By the late sixteenth century, however, the term was also being used in an archaic sense to mean 'battle'. In the O.E.D Edward Hall is cited to illustrate a shift of meaning of the word 'field' from battle to the assembling of forces: O.E.D. (1901), IV, i, 192.86.

26. See C.L. Kingsford (ed.), *Chronicles of London* (Oxford, 1905), 193 (B.L. Vitellius A XVI MS).

27. Hutton may have been influenced by the popular Bowen map of Leicestershire of 1756, which showed the ovoid area of 'King Ric:feld' as marked on Saxton and others, but designated as 'Radmore Plain'. Hutton does say that 'the whole field is uneven', meaning 'Redmore'. See Hutton, 69. For Bowen's map, see R.K. Baum, *Antique Maps of Leicestershire* (Loughborough, 1981), 7-8.

28. Ibid.

29. M. Drayton, *Poly-Olbion*, song XXII (1622), in J. William Hebel (ed.), *The Works of Michael Drayton* (Oxford, 1961), IV, 462.

30. This begins even with the *Crowland Chronicle* and 'The Rose of England' ballad; see C. Ross, *The Wars of the Roses* (London, 1976), 14.

31. Hutton, 68.

32. A.H. Burne, *The Battlefields of Britain* (London, 1950), 152. (hereafter, Burne).

33. Hutton's exact location of these 'earthworks' is a problem, because of his poor knowledge of the locality and his vague use of language. It may be that the zig-zag line referred to in connection with Henry's camp is the crooked parish boundary between Shenton and Sutton Cheney (see Hutton, 71-2; also 63).

34. Hutton, 50; *Crowland Chronicle*, 573-4: *Die autem Dominico ante festum Bartholomei Apostoli, Rex... opidum Leicestrense egressus* (Then on Sunday before the Feast of Saint Bartholomew the Apostle [24 August] the King marched out of the town of Leicester.)

35. See The Deserted Medieval Village Research Group, 'Provisional List of Deserted Medieval Villages in Leicestershire', *Trans. Leics. Arch. Hist. Soc.* XXXIX (1963-4), 25. Ambion may have been deserted as a result of shrinkage from the margins of the settlement in the second half of the fourteenth century. The earliest record of 'Anebein' is c.1270.

36. Hutton, 79-80.

37. On Pridden it is marked as a 'hillock'; see Nichols, 557.

38. P.J. Foss, 'The Sutton Cheney Estates: The Pre-Enclosure Landscape', *The Hinckley Historian*, XX (Autumn 1987), 19-26.

39. Hutton, 67, 69, 94.

40. Ibid., 126-7. 'Amyon Lays' was presumably part of the herd pasture in Sutton Cheney open fields in the late eighteenth century, on the north side of Ambion Hill. The western stretches of this pasture were called Cordley Furze, which was then largely scrub and waste (Hutton calls it Cornhill furze). Hutton also makes sure that his Richard 'rides out of the right flank', (p. 108) in order that he should arrive down from the hill to the north, although the small amount of evidence there is suggests the opposite (see Chapter Four).

41. Holinshed, 1420. See Hutton, iv.

42. Burne, 148-9.

43. See plans by R.F. Hartley, Jewry Wall Museum, Leicester. The wood on Ambion Hill ('but small' in the time of Robinson and Nichols) grew up as secondary woodland on the herd pasture probably in the mid-eighteenth century. Before then, Ambion would seem to have been scrub-land and former wood-pasture from the sixteenth century onwards.

44. The earliest reference to 'King Richard's Well' we find on a map of the prospective route of the Ashby canal, dated 1781, in Leicestershire Record Office DE 421/4/2,ii. In the 1784 Montague Estate survey of Sutton Cheney, there is mention of an 'Ambion Well' which may be the same.

45. Hutton, vii.

46. J. Throsby, *Select Views in Leicestershire* (London, 1789), I, 338.

47. Nichols, 556.

48. Ibid.

49. Plate LXXXIX, p.556. Pridden shows 'Radmore Plain' to be the area to the south of this meadow, between it and the Sence brook. In Nichols' note P it is given as 'commonly called Sutton Cow-pastures'. This was the Greenhill common, capped by a gravel outwash where the present-day Greenhill Farm

stands. It formed a portion of the herd-pasture on the west of Sutton parish, but is not a plain, and has never been called 'Redmore'. (See P.J. Foss, 'The Building-Accounts of Greenhill Farm, Sutton Cheney, 1795-97', *Aspect* (The Market Bosworth and District Magazine), XIV, no. 151 (April 1987).)

50. Nichols, 555.

51. Ibid., 557. This mistake was adopted by the surveyors of the First Series one-inch O.S. maps.

52. See P.J. Foss, 'The Sutton Cheney Estates: The Pre-Enclosure Landscape', op. cit. The Small Meadow, which followed the alluvial bed of a vanished tributary of the Sence Brook divided the two great fields of Sutton Cheney, called Little Field (or Pickmeadow Field) and Ambien Field.

53. Nichols, 549. Burton's annotated copy of his own book is in Staffordshire Record Office D649/4/1-3. The other two references are to a revised version of *The Description of Leicestershire* and to a publisher's mock-up of a projected second edition of 1642, which, however, never materialised. All three manuscripts differ, and it is not easy to say which is best, although clearly Burton intended his final version to be the 1642 mock-up. For the background and history of the manuscripts, see J. Simmons, Introduction to J. Nichols, *History and Antiquities of Leicestershire* (Wakefield, 1974), I, viii, and D.T. Williams, 'William Burton's 1642 Revised Edition of "The Description of Leicestershire"', *Trans. Leics. Arch. Hist. Soc.* L (1974-5), 30-60. Our view of the manuscripts is that the later editions are not necessarily the most definitive or complete. Certainly, Burton was dissatisfied with the rushed publication of his 1622 book, and the book suffers from errors of omission and stylistic peculiarities. The chief advantages of the later revisions are that they tidy up the style, and offer a more succinct presentation, but they strike me as drier, and they dispense with much of the anecdotal material in the first edition. A first edition, with relevant corrections, and with the comprehensive annotations Burton provided, might be a better book.

54. F. Drake, *Eboracum: The History and Antiquities of the City of York* (York, 1736), I, 120-1.

55. Harley 542 ff.31-3v, was first printed by Nichols, pp.551-3. It was further published by J. and T. Spencer (eds.), in *Leicestershire and Rutland Notes and Queries* I (April 1889-Jan.1891), 53-8.

56. Nichols, 559. See also, F. Skillington, 'Sir John Beaumont of Grace Dieu', *Trans. Leics. Arch. Hist. Soc.* XLVII (1971-2), 43-50. George Ashby's comments on Beaumont's poem in the transcription in Nichols are interesting in showing to what extent the eighteenth century perspective on the battle differed from that of the seventeenth century. Ashby was a local antiquary and acquaintance of Nichols'; his reading of Beaumont's poem queried the picture of the battle displayed in it, particularly the assumption that King Richard allowed his vanguard to engage first, intended to augment it, but chose instead to 'divert his course another way' in order to bring matters to a crisis in a personal assault on Henry's position. This position is shown to be in the rear of the main 'battel' (the vanguard). All these details correspond remarkably with recent thinking about the battle (*vide* Goodman), and may reflect a truer picture than that which is revealed in George Ashby's incredulous accompanying comments. Clearly, the eighteenth century view was that the battle was all of a piece, King Richard was involved in the main attack, and Henry was also in the forefront of the vanguard.

57. Nichols, plate XCII, p.557.

58. Ibid., 544.

59. J. Nichols, *The History and Antiquities of Hinckley* (London 1782), 17, 101.

60. See *White's Trade Directory* of 1846 and 1860, in the latter p.687.

61. J.F. Hollings, 'Scene of the Death of Richard III', *Notes and Queries,* 2nd ser., VI, no.150 (18 November 1858), 392.

62. J. Gairdner, 'The Battle of Bosworth', *Archaeologia* LV, i (1896), 177. Hollings' conjecture was based on a serious misunderstanding as to the line of the Mancetter to Leicester Roman road which he seems to have confused with the modern Shenton to Sutton road. This fact, together with Hollings' arbitrary consultation with three local farmers, and his statement concerning the rights of Shenton people to take sand from Ambion Hill in a period before the 1789 enclosure of Sutton Cheney, can hardly be considered well-founded evidence on which to base a theory about the location of the fifteenth century Sandeford. In addition, Hollings never calls this location the 'Sandeford', but specifically refers to it as the *Water Gate* in the nineteenth century. So far there is no evidence from the Sutton or Shenton records of the eighteenth

and nineteenth centuries to substantiate the tradition concerning the use of sand from the Ambion Pit by Shenton parishioners, although this may have been an unwritten agreement.

63. A Leicestershire County Council notice-board erected near Sutton brook in about 1974, states 'This is the place known as the Sandeford, where Richard III was killed at Bosworth fight.' It then rehearses the story we find in Hollings about the sand pit on Ambion Hill. However, none of this is substantiated by any historical evidence, and to say that this spot was known as the Sandeford in the fifteenth (or in any) century is clearly misleading.

64. H.J. Francis, MS Notebook on the Battle of Bosworth Field (c. 1910), Hinckley Library Local History Collection Box 3, p.58.

65. A.J. Pickering, *Footpath Rambles Around Hinckley* (Hinckley: Pickering and Son, 1929), 13. For another local view, reiterating the same errors and myths created by Hutton and Hollings, see J.T. Burgess, *The Last Battle of the Roses: A Paper on the Battle of Bosworth Field* (Leamington, 1872), 21.

66. D.T. Williams, *The Battle of Bosworth* (Leicester, 1973), 23.

67. Ibid., 8.

68. See especially, A. Goodman, *The Wars of the Roses: Military Activity and English Society 1452-97* (London, 1981); C. Richmond, 'The Battle of Bosworth', *History Today* (August 1985); O.D. Harris, 'The Bosworth Commemoration at Dadlington', *The Ricardian* VII, no. 90 (September 1985) and '"Even here in Bosworth Field": A Disputed Site of Battle', *The Ricardian* VII, no. 92 (March 1986); and R.A. Griffiths and R.S. Thomas, *The Making of the Tudor Dynasty* (Gloucester, 1985).

69. P.J. Foss, 'The Field of Redemore', *Aspect* (The Market Bosworth and District Magazine), XIII, nos. 135-143 (November 1985-July 1986); 'The Site of the Battle of Bosworth', Research Notes and Queries, *The Ricardian* VII, no. 98 (September, 1987), 486-7; 'A Significant Document: The Hinckley-Lyre Agreement (1283) and the Site of the Battle of Bosworth', *The Hinckley Historian* 22 (Autumn, 1988).

Chapter Three

1. William Burton was born at Lindley, $2^1/_2$ miles from Stoke Golding, in 1575. After a career in law in London, he lived in premature retirement at one of the family seats, Falde in Staffordshire, from where he published his life's work, *The Description of Leicestershire* in 1622. In 1623 he returned to Lindley, where he worked steadily on revisions of his book up to 1644, the date of the final corrections of the revised edition. He seems to have returned to Falde in about 1642, and died there in 1645. His father, Ralph Burton, purchased the manor of Dadlington in 1585, and bequeathed it to his son.

2. W. Burton, *The Description of Leicestershire* (London, 1622), 82. (hereafter, Burton).

3. See letter dated 25 July 1638 to Sir Simon D'Ewes, B.L. Harley 374/63.

4. Burton, 47.

5. Ibid. This information remains in all three versions of the manuscript of the book, although the wording is altered for clarity's sake.

6. The earliest enclosure in Market Bosworth was taking place in the 1580s, and was completed by c.1630; in Cadeby, enclosure was already complete by 1597. There are no records of finds associated with the battle of Bosworth in either of these parishes; see P.J. Foss, *The History of Market Bosworth* (Wymondham, 1983), 28.

7. G.F. Farnham, 'Stoke Golding: Manorial History', *Trans. Leics. Arch. Hist. Soc.* XIV, ii (1926), 206-227. The sale was effected in 1605.

8. Burton, 47.

9. Hales and Furnivall, III, 252.

10. Ibid., 253.

11. Ibid., 359.

12. Nichols, 553.

13. J.O. Halliwell (ed.), *The Most Pleasant Song of Lady Bessye* (Percy Society, London, 1847), 75.

14. Nichols, 552.

15. Hales and Furnivall, III, 252.

16. Ibid., 361.

17. Contained in the York House Book B2-4, City of York Archives, Exhibition Square, York. See R. Davies, *Extracts from the Municipal Records of the City of York in the Reigns of Edward IV, Edward V, and Richard III* (London, 1843). (hereafter, Davies).

18. Davies, 214-5.

19. Ibid., 216. Davies mistakes 'Beskwood' (Bestwood Lodge) for 'Prestwould'. Gairdner implies that Richard used Bestwood for his day's sojourn and for hunting, whilst probably returning to Nottingham Castle at night. See J. Gairdner, *History of the Life and Reign of Richard III* (Cambridge, 1898), 232 n. The king knew of the landing of Henry Tudor by the 11 August, since he sent a letter of muster from Bestwood to Henry Vernon of Haddon, Derbyshire, to bring his quota of men-at-arms, 'sufficiently horsed and harnessed'. See C. Ross, *Richard III* (London, 1981), 211.

20. Davies, 218.

21. That soldiers did travel to battlefields by horse is confirmed by Dominic Mancini in 1483. It was the custom for English soldiers to travel by horse but fight on foot. (See C.A.J. Armstrong, *The Usurpation of Richard III by Dominic Mancini* (Oxford, 1969), 98-100).   –

22. Davies, 217. Davies's transcription gives Redemore as 'Rodemore', undoubtedly a misreading of the text of f.169. This is repeated by Angelo Raine in *York Civic Records* I (York 1939), 118. (My own reading of the text is confirmed by Dr. Lorraine Attreed in pers. comm.)

23. College of Arms MS 2M6 ff.55r-60r. See R.Firth Green, 'Historical Notes of a London Citizen, 1483-1488', *Eng.Hist.Rev.* XCVI, no.380 (July 1981), 585-90. The manuscript is ascribed to c.1513, although considered to be an authentic copy of a contemporary set of annals.

24. This reference, previously unnoticed, was discovered by myself and T.V.Parry in the National Library of Scotland (Ref: C.7.b.11). In the margin of folio ccxxvii of the copy of Fabyan's *Chronicle* of 1533 (previously in the Advocates Library, Scotland), is the note (slightly pared away): 'the battay[le] of Redesmore heath was bytwene K.R. & K.H. th[e] vijth'. 'Redesmore' would indicate a derivation from *hreodes mor*, literally 'the moor of the reeds'.

25. A.Hanham, *Richard III and his Early Historians* (Oxford, 1975), 58-9; see also Bennett, 14.

26. Fabyan, f.ccxxx.

27. See H.Ellis (ed.), *Three Books of Polydore Vergil's English History,* Camden Society XXIX (1844), 225. M.Condon, 'Bosworth Field: A Footnote to a Controversy', *The Ricardian* VII, no. 96 (January 1987), 365, n2. John Leland referred to Towton as 'Palmesunday feld'; see L. Toulmin Smith (ed.), *Leland's Itinerary in England and Wales* (London, 1964), II, 18.

28. *Crowland Chronicle,* 575. Bennett makes this point too in his *Battle of Bosworth,* 14.

29. *ad octo miliaria ab eo opido distantia, juxta Abbathiam de Mirivall. Crowland Chronicle,* 574. Merevale Abbey is 20 statute miles from Leicester.

30. John Rous's account is published in T.Hearne (ed.), *Historia Johannis Rossi Warwicensis de Regibus Anglie* (London, 1716), 218.

31. See A.Hanham, *Richard III and his Early Historians* op. cit., 107. The manuscript is Bodley Ashmole 1448, f.275.

32. O.D.Harris, '"...Even here, in Bosworth Field": A Disputed Site of Battle', *The Ricardian* VII, no.92 (March 1986), 198.

33. For details of this document, see Appendix II.

34. I am indebted to Tim Parry for his help in locating a transcription of the Latin text of this document, and to the Richard III and Yorkist History Trust for funding research in France. See P.J. Foss, 'A Significant Document: The Hinckley-Lyre Agreement (1283) and the Site of the Battle of Bosworth', *The Hinckley Historian* 22 (Autumn, 1988).

35. The valley is still subject to flooding on occasions today, despite centuries of drainage. See Plate 10

36. Evidence for the shrinkage of settlement from the margins of parishes in West Leicestershire is exemplified by the abandonment of Ambion between 1350 and 1400. See The Deserted Medieval Village Research Group, 'Provisional List of Deserted Medieval Villages in Leicestershire', *Trans. Leics. Arch. Hist. Soc.* XXXIX (1963-4), 25.

37. See G.F. Farnham, 'Stoke Golding Manorial History', *Trans. Leics. Arch. Hist. Soc.* XIV, ii (1926), 208. References to 'Siddwell close' in a deed of 1605 in the Baxter papers at Sheffield City Library, Box 4, 60787/3 locates the earlier 'Segwelle'. An open stretch of water would seem to have existed here up to the eighteenth century, when maps of the Ashby-de-la-Zouch canal company mark a 'Bath' (that is a large pool) in the cleft of the valley. See Ashby canal company map (1793), Leicestershire Record Office, Q.S.72/2. Adjacent closes in Dadlington parish were called Bath meadows.

38. M. Gelling, *Place-Names in the Landscape* (London, 1984), 41ff.

39. 'Fenmore Close' is traceable back to 1709; see W.T. Hall, *Notes for a History of Dadlington* (the author, 1942). 40. O. Rackham, *The History of the Countryside* (London, 1986), 353-5.

41. The name is marked 'Foomeers' on the 1835 O.S. map and is likely to be derived from 'Ful maere' (= foul mere), see J. Field, *English Field Names* (Newton Abbot, 1972), 81. The name is recorded as early as 1727 on a map of Shenton lordship made for the Wollaston estate by Robert Cushee (Leicestershire Record Office 6D43/31). This probably corresponds with 'le Fennes' mentioned in an Inquisition Post Mortem of Richard Everard of Shenton, dated 1593. See G.F. Farnham, *Leicestershire Medieval Village Notes* IV (Leicester, 1930), 68.

42. Again marked on Cushee's map of 1727 as 'the Great Moorey leyes' (see reference above). A farmhouse of eighteenth century construction stood in Dadlington parish to the south of this moorland at SP388981, and known since 1713 as Dadlington Fenns Farm.

43. The ridge and furrow in Leicestershire has been mapped by Mr. R.F. Hartley of Leicestershire Museums. See 'Aerial Archaeology in Leicestershire', *Midlands Prehistory*, ed. A. Gibson (BAR 204, 1989), 96

44. Heathland was common in medieval times in much of the bare upland terrain of west Leicestershire, but in association with wetland only in the flatland adjacent to the Fenn Lanes. Closes called 'heathe' and 'fen holes' in the west of Stoke and Dadlington parishes are found in title deeds relating to the sixteenth century Davill estate, among the Baxter papers in Sheffield City Library (see note 37).

45. C. Fox-Strangeways, *The Geology of the Country Between Atherstone and Charnwood Forest: Memoir of the British Geological Survey* (London, 1900), 40. Fox-Strangeways' conclusions are endorsed and updated by B.C. Worssam and R.A. Old, *Geology of the Country around Coalville: Memoir of the British Geological Survey* (1988), 305-9.

46. Dr. Robin Old, pers. comm. This seems to have been the case at Freizeland, west of Market Bosworth, mapped as Lacustrine Alluvium on Sheet 55: Coalville, 1: 50 000; Solid and Drift edition (British Geological Survey, 1982).

47. This shift of alignment is more pronounced on older maps and corresponds exactly with the band of alluvium at this point, SP 393 986. Such causeways across marshland were common in Roman times; see C.Taylor, *Roads and Tracks of Britain* (London, 1979), 76-7.

48. 'Even when water is permanently present, and free from much flow, the terrain remains free of bog development because its mineral base is so rich that there is plenty of microbial activity and any peat material is readily decomposed.' R. North, *Wild Britain* (London, 1983), 90 ff.

49. Ibid., 94.

50. Interestingly, one of the few Sites of Special Scientific Interest so designated by the Nature Conservancy Council in the Central English Midlands, exists in the valley between Dadlington and Stoke Golding. This is now called Kendall's Meadow, and is described in the NCC's report as 'a traditionally managed hay meadow with a diversity and richness of plant life unmatched in the south west of the County.'

51. See E. Ekwall, *The Concise Oxford Dictionary of English Place Names* (Oxford, 1980), 245-6.

52. R. Millward and A. Robinson, *The West Midlands* (London, 1971), 161 ff.

53. Mercian Mudstone is a new term for Keuper Marl.

54. Many of the nineteenth century field names indicate this kind of terrain: obviously, the Fenmores and the Fomers, but also the Great Moorey Leyes, the Great Moorey Leyes Meads and the Rushy and Gorsey closes in Shenton and Upton lordships, bordering the area of the Redemore.

55. F. Drake, Eboracum; *The History and Antiquities of the City of York* (York, 1736), 122; P.L. Hughes and J.F. Larkin (eds.), *Tudor Royal Proclamations* I (New Haven, 1964), 3.

56. Davies, 218.

57. Without any documentary clue as to the whereabouts of a Sandeford at any period, the identification can only be speculative. The nearest such place-name to the site of the battle that I have been able to find dating from the Middle Ages is 'Sandforde' located west of Wolvey Heath, in a document quoted in Dugdale (cited in the *Victoria County History for Warwickshire,* VI, 282). This may be identified with the fields called Sandyford in Burton Hastings, adjacent to the crossing of a tributary of the upper Soar near Leicester Grange, SP 435 901. If so, the topography and geographical conditions are very similar to the pattern found in other ancient 'Sandfords'.

58. M. Gelling, *The Place Names of Berkshire* II (London, 1974), 431. Margaret Gelling discussed this derivation in a seminar at Nottingham University, 24 October 1987. See also J. Field, *Place-Names of Great Britain and Ireland* (Newton Abbot, 1980).

59. After 1670.

60. Evidenced by soil borings undertaken in 1986. Information also from Mr. R. Burgess, Lodge Farm, Dadlington.

61. The name is first given on the 1843 Dadlington tithe map.

62. J.S. Brewer, *Letters and Papers, Foreign and Domestic, of the Reign of Henry VIII,* I, ii (London, 1862), 279.

63. For the complete text, see O.D. Harris, 'The Bosworth Commemoration at Dadlington', *The Ricardian* VII, no.90 (September 1985), 124.

64. T.V. Parry, *A Church for Bosworth Field,* (the author, 1987), 7. Information endorsed by H.M. Colvin of Oxford.

65. See Harris, op. cit., 125-6; and Parry, ibid., 16-17.

66. Harris, ibid., Appendix 1B, p.125. W.A. Jackson, 'Three Printed English Indulgences at Harvard', *Harvard Library Bulletin* VII (1953), 229-31.

67. That Richard III attended Mass in Sutton Cheney church is highly unlikely, given the sources and traditions of the battle. This may have originated at the time of the foundation of the Fellowship of the White Boar in 1924. The use and abuse of spurious tradition has had unfortunate consequences in the locality: for example, the eradication of long-established local names, such as that of 'The Greyhound Inn', Sutton Cheney, (first mentioned in c. 1820) and its replacement by the name 'Royal Arms'.

Chapter Four

1. R.A. Griffiths and R.S. Thomas, *The Making of the Tudor Dynasty* (Gloucester, 1985), 144, 146-7.

2. In particular, Rhys ap Thomas, whose prowess is praised in the Stanley ballads. See Emyr Wyn Jones, *Bosworth Field... A Welsh Retrospect* (Liverpool and Llandewi Brefi, 1984), 24-33; and D. Rees, *The Son of Prophecy: Henry Tudor's Road to Bosworth* (London, 1985), 110-16.

3. Vergil writes in his manuscript of '*Haaberhystwyath, quae praesidio ab adversariis non firmo tenebatur. Hanc Henricus oppugnare aggressus haud multo labore cepit.*' See Hay, 207.

4. The story of Thomas Mitton's actions as mayor of Shrewsbury is told in *The Rose of Englande.* See Hales and Furnivall, 192-3.

5. *tamen in timore non paruo erat.* Polydore Vergil, 554.

6. A. Goodman, *The Wars of the Roses: Military Activity and English Society 1452-97* (London, 1981), 91.

7. This is Harris's view; see O.D. Harris,"'... even here in Bosworth Field': a Disputed Site of Battle", *The Ricardian* VII, no. 92 (March 1986), 196.

8. Nichols, 552. In the Stow MS the distinction is drawn between the Sunday (21 August) on which the Stanleys heard mass in Atherstone, and the evening before when Sir William Stanley arrived there.

9. W.Campbell (ed.), *Materials for a History of the Reign of Henry VII* (Rolls Series 1873), I, 201. The date of the order is 7 December 1485.

10. Merevale Abbey possessed the churches of Baxterley, Grendon, Weston and Orton-on-the-Hill and built granges at Newhouse, Lea, Moorbarn and Pinwall, the latter very close to Atherstone. The tradition in Atherstone is that a meadow $^1/_2$ mile north of the town was the site of the 'royal' camp at SP985315. This is marked 'Royal Meadow' on a pre-enclosure map of Atherstone dated 1716 (*A Plan of Atherston Feildes... by Robt. Hewitt*, Warwicks. Rec. Office, P.7).

11. Hall, f.xxviii.

12. Hales and Furnivall, 251. The Watling Street crosses the Anker at Witherley. Wooded landscape – part of the Forest of Arden – was a distinctive feature of the north Warwickshire country in the Middle Ages. The landscape of west Leicestershire, on the other hand, seems to have been a bare, rolling upland since long before Domesday. A glance at statistical maps in H.C. Darby, *Domesday England* (Cambridge, 1977), 183,and in O. Rackham, *Trees and Woodland in the British Landscape* (Dent, 1976), 62, will confirm this.

13. J. Gairdner, *History of the Life and Reign of Richard III* (Cambridge, 1898), 364. The Harley 78 MS f.31 is a French-written document of c.1529. It records knights made by Henry VII before and after the battle, some of which were apparently published by Writhe, Garter King of Arms. The meeting of Henry and Stanley is described in Hall, f.xxx as taking place 'in a lytle close', which might have been the Roman encampment of Manduessedum on the Watling Street, on the right hand side of the River Anker, and still by then a noticeable feature of the landscape.

14. Margaret Gelling has pointed out that the dense scatter of 'tun'-names among the hamlets of west Leicestershire indicate settlement in the period from 750 to 950 AD in unwooded upland, formerly wood-pasture. Sixteenth century writers frequently remarked that the battle was fought among the villages ending in '-tun'. See M. Gelling, 'The Evidence of Place-Names 1', in P.H. Sawyer (ed.), *English Medieval Settlement* (Arnold, 1979); and W. Burton in his MS annotations, in Nichols, 549.

15. Nichols, 646.

16. Polydore Vergil, 556. Vergil's words are *Henricus... propius hostes castra ponit.* Hales and Furnivall, 251. The Stow MS., abbreviating the course of events, refers to King Henry asking the vanward of the Lord Stanley 'on the morrow, when the larke gan synge'. I take this to indicate the request by Henry before the battle to have Lord Stanley's forces join with his, as reported in Vergil's account. There, Stanley is said to hold his position detached and midway, saying that he will come to Henry's aid when he is ready; however it is likely that arrangements had been made for some contingents to reinforce Henry's army - very likely those forces under the four knights mentioned in *Bosworth Feilde;* Hales and Furnivall, 252.

17. W. Campbell, *Materials... of the Reign of Henry VII* (Rolls Series, 1873), I, 188, 201. The wording of the document is significant; it speaks of 'certaine townships, which susteygned losses of their cornes & graynes by us and oure companye at oure late victorious feld'. Atherstone received £20 and a further £4-13s-4d., and Fenny Drayton also £20. The other villages received considerably less. It has been suggested (by D. Starkey, 'Or Merevale?', *History Today* XXXV (October 1985)) that the wording indicates a site of battle nearer to Atherstone, but as I argue, the document seems to refer to foraging, not destruction in the course of the battle, and the quantity of the garnering in the parish of Drayton may indicate the last stage of the journey before striking camp on the moor at the eastern extremity of Fenny Drayton.

18. See Note 9.

19. Lord Stanley had to be in sight of, and within reach of, Henry's position, to co-ordinate strategy; this is one argument against the unlikely position of the Stanley forces on the hills to the north of Ambion, where they would have been too distant from Henry's army. See C. Ross, *Richard III* (London, 1981), 217n.; S.B. Chrimes, *Henry VII* (London, 1972), 47.

20. The discovery by the king of the plot involving Lord Strange, Sir William Stanley and Sir John Savage is recorded in the *Crowland Chronicle*, 573. Sir William Stanley was publicly denounced traitor in Coventry and elsewhere about the time he was collaborating with Henry from Shrewsbury onwards. The ballads

make much of the fact that Sir William Stanley had promised to provide 'such a breakeffast' to King Richard 'as never subiect did to Kinge'. *Ladye Bessiye,* Hales and Furnivall, 355. See also *Bosworth Feilde,* ibid, 256.

21. Hales and Furnivall, 250; repeated in the Stow MS, Nichols, IV, 552. Sir Edward Stanley, Sir William's son, is said to be on the wing.

22. Hales and Furnivall, 252. The fact that these men joined the main 'battle' (that is, what was in effect the vanguard) is known by the later role played by Sir John Savage on the left wing of Henry's advance formation. The *Ladye Bessiye* tradition also mentions Savage in this role, and states that Sir William Stanley was intended by Lord Thomas to be 'in that battell'. This intermingling of contingents from the Stanley forces may explain later (though corrupt) variants, where Stanley is seen as a participating force in the main battle. However, the ballad tradition (which would be naturally favourable to Stanley's role) does not say this; Lord Stanley is said to 'hover on this hill' (Hales and Furnivall, 259), and Vergil states that Thomas Stanley *ut medius loco hostes appropinquarat.* (Polydore Vergil, 556). Sir John Beaumont's poem is interesting in this respect in that it suggests that Lord Stanley aided Henry secretly with a small contingent whilst the main army remained with Sir William Stanley (see A.B.Grosart (ed.), *Poems of Sir John Beaumont* (1869), 44). The confusion on this score may have been helped by Hall's mistranslation of Vergil's line about Henry 'relying on the aid of the Lord Stanley', *ipse autem fretus auxilio Thomae Stanlei:* Polydore Vergil, 556. Hall, f.XXX, gives it as 'with the aide of ye Lord Stanley'.

23. These two locations are the only logical positions for the Stanley forces given the consensus of evidence that exists. Interestingly, a later local tradition associates an area south-west of Stoke Golding with the Stanley forces - a field later named 'The Big Dining Room' at SP 387 965. See W.T.Hall, *A Collection for a History of Stoke Golding* (the author, 1928).

24. G.Doutrepont and O. Jodogne (eds.), *Chroniques de Jean Molinet* I, 1474-88, (Brussels, 1935), 435. (Hereafter, Jean Molinet).

25. See A. Goodman and A. Mackay, 'A Castilian Report on English Affairs, 1486', *Eng. Hist. Rev.* LXXX (1973) p.96. This is supported to some extent by the (later) Scottish tradition embodied in Pittscottie's *Chronicles* dating from the 1570s. See A.J.G. Mackay (ed.), *The History and Chronicles of Scotland from the Slaughter of King James the First to the Ane Thousande Fyve Hundreith Thrie Scoir Fyftein Yeir, written and Collected by Robert Lindesay of Pittscottie* (Scottish Text Society, 1899-1911), I, 190-0.

26. Pittscottie notes that Lord Stanley was 'a great part of King Richard's vanguard' and during the battle turned round and faced King Richard 'as if they had been his enemies'. See A.J.G. Mackay, *Pittscottie's Chronicle... op.cit.*

27. C. Ross, *Richard III* (London, 1981), 220.

28. *aciem instruit simplicem;* Polydore Vergil, 556.

29. *in dextero cornu aciei locat Gilbertum Talbotum, qui id tueatur, in sinistro vero ponit Ioannem Sauagium.* Polydore Vergil, 556.

30. D. Hay, *The 'Anglica Historia' of Polydore Vergil 1485-1537* (Camden Society Ser. LXXIV, 1950), 24-5, 96-7.

31. Bennett, 7.

32. *Ita utrinque instructa acie, ubi procul inter se milites conspicere potuerunt, sese galeis armant, atque ad pugnam parant.* Polydore Vergil, 556.

33. See Bennett, 165.

34. See R.A. Griffiths and R.S. Thomas, *The Making of the Tudor Dynasty* (Gloucester, 1985), 161. Jean Molinet, 435: *Les Francois pareillement firent leurs preparations en marchans contre les Englez, estant aux champz a ung quart de lieue.*

35. *Inter utrunque exercitum intercedebat palus, quam Henricus de industria ad dexteram dimisit, ut suis instar munimente esset: simul etiam id faciendo, solem a tergo reliquit.* Polydore Vergil, 556. Makinson chose to suggest Vergil confused his left hand with his right hand, and put the marsh on the opposite side of Henry's forces. This suits the logics of his conjecture, but this is an unacceptable use of historiographical data; see A. Makinson. 'The Road to Bosworth Field, August 1485', *History Today* (April 1963), 247.

36. D.T. Williams, '"A place Mete for twoo battayles to encountre": the Siting of the Battle of Bosworth, 1485', *The Ricardian* VII, no.90 (September 1985), 88-9.

37. Jean Molinet, 435.

38. Hales and Furnivall, 194.

39. *les Franchois, cognoissans par le trait du roy la situation du lieu et maniere de sa bataille...* Jean Molinet, 435.

40. Vegetius, *De Re Militari*, Book III, Chapter 20; Christine de Pisan's adaptation of Vegetius contained in the *Fayttes of Armes* was a favourite text of Henry VII and was given to Caxton to translate. It was delivered to him, according to Caxton's *Epilogue*, by the Earl of Oxford. See A.T.P. Byles (ed.), *The Book of Fayttes of Armes and of Chyvalrye* (1408-9), (Oxford Early English Text Society, 1932), 291.

41. *Crowland Chronicle*, 574.

42. Jean Molinet, 435; *Crowland Chronicle*, 574: *Denique ingrentibus moderato passu Principe & militibus partis adversae super exercitum Regis...*

43. *Rex maxima pompa diadema portans in capite, cum Duce Norfolchiae Johanne de Howard, ac Henrico Percy Comite Northumbriae..: Crowland Chronicle*, 573.

44. Vergil, 554, actually describes the king marching in the midst of his army with the armaments, *en route* from Nottingham to Leicester.

45. M.Drayton, *Poly-Olbion*, Song XXII (1622), in J. William Hebel (ed.), *The Works of Michael Drayton* (Oxford, 1961), IV, 462; this corresponds with the suggestion in the *Crowland Chronicle*, 574, that the Earl of Northumberland's army was positioned where there was no sign of opposition 'either in the giving or receiving of blows of war' - the term *in eo vero loco* does indicate a particular position at a distance from the main arena of fighting: *in eo vero loco ubi Comes Northumbriae cum satis decenti ingentique militia stabat, nihil adversi neque datis neque susceptis belli ictibus cernebatur*. See also the corresponding clue which is likely to refer to Northumberland in Fabyan's *Chronicle*, f.CCXXX: 'And some stode houynge a ferre of/ tyll they sawe to whiche partye victory fyll.' Colin Richmond in his article 'The Battle of Bosworth', *History Today* (August 1985), 22, has some interesting points to make about the discrepancy between the sources' accounts of Norfolk's and Northumberland's formations on the wings, and the order of their approach to the battlefield. He suggests a way in which these might be reconciled.

46. C. Billson, *Medieval Leicester* (Leicester, 1920), 180ff.

47. For the direction of the Roman road, see A.D. McWhirr, 'The Roman Road from Leicester to Mancetter', *Trans. Leics. Arch. Hist. Soc.*, XLII (1966-7), 1-5; for medieval Leicester Forest, see L.Fox and P. Russell, *Leicester Forest* (Leicester, 1948).

48. P.J. Foss, 'The Sutton Cheney Estates: The Pre-Enclosure Landscape', *Hinckley Historian* 20 (Autumn 1987), 19-26. Eastward, this road would have followed the present Earl Shilton to Croft road; westward, there still remains a track to Stapleton brockey. Beyond this, the route can only be picked up on the Sutton Cheney enclosure map of 1797, where it is marked as 'Leicester Lane'; it coincides with the boundaries of old enclosures in Sutton. North-west of Ambion it is picked up by the boundary of Shenton parish, an old mere, and still further north-west by the A444 and then the Salt Lane, which is also the county boundary, in Appleby Magna. For this, see R.Dunmore, 'Appleby Magna's County Boundaries', The *Hinckley Historian* 19 (Spring 1987), 27-8.

49. The name 'King Richard's Well' occurs on a map of the Ashby canal company of 1781, although it was also known locally as 'Ambion Well' in the 1780s, as shown by a Dixie Estate Survey of 1788 (Leics. Rec. Office DE 40/22/4). There are in fact, several springs on Ambion Hill; and the cairn of 1813, erected by Samuel Parr, does not necessarily locate the spring traditional to Richard III in the eighteenth century.

50. Hutton, 97; C. Ross, *Richard III* (London, 1981), 220; D.T. Williams, '"A place mete for twoo battayles to encountre": the siting of the Battle of Bosworth', *The Ricardian* VII, no.90 (September 1985), 94. See also the plan in P.M. Kendall, *Richard III* (London, 1955), 362-3.

51. *Ricardus... cuncto exercitu ex castris educto, aciem dirigit mirabili longitudine productam.* Polydore Vergil, 555.

52. A.Goodman, *The Wars of the Roses: Military Activity and English Society 1452-97* (London, 1981), 93.

53. *Comes autem Oxoniae... in eam alam ubi Dux Norfolchiae constitutus erat, magno tam Gallicorum quam Anglicorum comitatu stipatus tetendit. Crowland Chronicle,* 574.

54. Hales and Furnivall, 361.

55. Vergil's phrase is *confertis manipulis,* 'in a closely-packed company' (p.556). In fact, fearing his small company might be surrounded by the multitude of the enemy, Oxford ordered that they should close themselves around the standards. This had the added result of confusing the enemy as to his intentions and enabling a pause in the attack.

56. H. Ellis (ed.), *Three Books of Polydore Vergil's English History* (Camden Society, 1844), 224.

57. Hales and Furnivall, 359.

58. Polydore Vergil, 556. It is important to note that Vergil distinguishes between the actions of Oxford 'on his part' and the actions of the others on theirs.

59. Hales and Furnivall, 361. Vergil's phrase for the wedge-formation is *facto cuneo,* which can also be translated 'in the formation of a column'.

60. Goodman makes the point that the failure to show an example in the execution of Lord Strange was in marked contrast to Edward IV's execution of Lord Welles before the Battle of Lose-Coat Field in 1470, and bespeaks confusion and lack of authority in Richard's camp. See A. Goodman, op. cit., 95.

61. See note 45 above. The meaning of the line is slightly ambiguous, although Bennett's translation (p.157) is preferable to those of Ellis and Pronay. The word *cernebatur* puts the emphasis on there being no *sign* of contest rather than on no activity of battle.

62. That is, if Richard was still doubtful about Lord Stanley's commitment; according to our interpretation, Stanley held the balance of power on the southern side of the battlefield. Sir John Beaumont's poem does suggest that it was Richard's intention to support the vanguard when he is told of the isolation of Richmond's position covered by the shade of a hill. He then diverts his course 'another way' and ascends the rising ground to see Henry better:

> The King intended, at his setting out,
> To helpe his vantguard; but a nimble scout
> Runnes crying, Sir, I saw not farre from hence,
> Where Richmond houers with a small defence,
> And like one guilty of some heynous ill,
> Is cover'd with the shade of yonder hill
> . . . .
> He now diverts his course another way
> And with his army led in faire array,
> Ascends the rising ground, and taking view
> of Henrie's army, sees they are but few.....

(A.B.Grosart (ed.), *Poems of Sir John Beaumont* (private circ., 1869), 52.)

63. *Ricardus primo a speculatoribus procul Henricum paucis stipatum armatis esse intelligit, deinde iam propius accedentem, certius ex signis Henricum cognoscit, qui tum inflammatus ira, concitat calcaribus equum, atque in eum ex altero latere ultra acies incurrit.* Richard first receives intelligence through his spies, then he ascertains for himself more clearly by drawing nearer. Polydore Vergil, 556.

64. *Ex altero latere ultra acies incurrit.* The line has been mis-translated many times, most notably by Hall and the sixteenth century translator of Vergil. See H.Ellis, *Three Books of Polydore Vergil's English History* (Camden Society, 1844), 224.

65. Note here Vergil's word *descendit* on p.557. These actions are of course supported by the ballad tradition, whereby Richard calls for his battle-axe and his crown and charges into the fray.

66. 'in a marris' occurs only in the Stow MS (Harley 542) version of *Bosworth Feilde;* see Nichols, 553; so does 'downe at a banke'.

67. E.M.Nokes and G.Wheeler, 'A Spanish Account of the Battle of Bosworth', *The Ricardian* II no.36 (March 1972), 2.

68. *equum velocem adduxerunt,* Polydore Vergil, 557; Hales and Furnivall, 257.

69. In other words, Richard used the horse to go into battle; but perhaps there were two horses involved, one a swift horse for escape, the other his war-horse. There is an interesting sixteenth century carved misericord at Christchurch Priory in Hampshire, depicting Richard III wielding his battle-axe. (See illustration in C.Ross, *The Wars of the Roses* (London, 1976), 8).

70. Jean Molinet, 435: *son cheval saulta en ung palus duquel ne se pooit ravoir; et lors fut approchiet d'ung de ceulx de Gales qui, d'une halebarde, l'abbaty mort.* The fifteenth century Welsh poet, Guto'r Glyn, in a cywydd written in praise of Sir Rhys ap Thomas, intimates that he was the one who killed Richard III. The line 'Lladd y baedd, eilliodd ei ben' can be translated 'Killed the boar, destroyed his head.' (See I.Williams and J.Ll.Williams, *Gwaith Guto'r Glyn* (Cardiff: University of Wales Press, 1939), 264.) There is also a tradition that Rhys Fawr ap Meredydd of Hiraethog was responsible for the death of the king; see E.W.Jones, *Bosworth Field...A Welsh Retrospect* (Liverpool and Llandewi Brefi, 1984) for these various traditions. It has been claimed (by D.T.Williams in a riposte in *History Today* XXXV (October 1985)), that there was a 'well-authenticated tradition of the last decade of the fifteenth century that Richard III was killed in a stream or ditch'. Presumably, this view is based on a fragment of Welsh bardic tradition, where a prophetic ode of Dyfydd Llwyd of Mathafarn describes Henry Tudor's worthiness in being the one to kill Richard III 'like a dog slain in a ditch'. Apart from this being a simile as well as a prophetic wish, the translation (to be found in P.Tudor-Craig's *Richard III Catalogue* (Boydell, 1973), 95) should perhaps more correctly read 'hedge' rather than 'ditch'. The Welsh line is 'Y ci a las yn y clawdd': see W.L.Richards (ed.), *Gwaith Dafydd Llwyd o Fathatharn* (Cardiff: University of Wales Press, 1964), 70.) There is one other similar reference to a ditch (dyke) in one of the minutes of the York municipality. Here a case was heard on 14 May 1491 against a man slandering the name of Richard III. The operative phrase records that one master Burton was heard to say 'that kyng Richard was an ypocryte a crochebake & beried in a dike like a dogge' (See R.Freedman, *Richard III and the City of York* (York City Archives, 1983), 17 - the reference is to House Book B7, f.39). In all, then, hardly a well-authenticated tradition! In fact, the substantive evidence seems to be that Richard was killed in a marsh or a bog. Molinet's phrase *en fange et en bedare* - in mud and filth- seems to reflect this, and is also echoed by the *Great Chronicle's* 'all to besprung wyth myrr & ffylth' (p.238).

71. C.Ross, *The Wars of the Roses* (London, 1976), 135.

72. Polydore Vergil, 557. *atque nullo accepto detrimento, abierunt* suggests they were allowed to escape if their desertion brought about the defeat of the king.

73. *quorum bene magnus numerus in ipsa fuga cecidit.* Polydore Vergil, 557. Williams suggests that Vergil describes Crown Hill as the furthest extent of the rout. This is clearly not so, although it fits in with Williams' idea that the rout went to the south. This follows Hutton and is reflected in Leicestershire County Council's interpretation, but of course is without authority. (See Note 36.)

74. *coronam Ricardi inter spolia repertam:* Polydore Vergil, 557.

75. This was first pointed out by K.B.MacFarlane reviewing *Calender of Entries in the Papal Registers XIV* (1960) in *Eng. Hist. Rev.* LXXVIII (1963), 771-2. It is discussed by A.Hanham in *Richard III and His Early Historians* (Oxford, 1975), 134. The text, however, seems to imply that Stanley, then Earl of Derby, confirmed that he had known his son-in-law well only since then, which may suggest that he had in fact met him briefly before.

76. *The Great Chronicle,* 238.

77. This is evidenced by the deed of sale of the Harrington estate dated 1605, referred to in Chapter III note 37.

78. J.Nichols, *History and Antiquities of Hinckley* (London, 1782), 100-1.

79. Harley 542 describes the body being taken to the New Warke for display; whilst Vergil records its burial at the Franciscans (p.558).

80. See D.Baldwin, 'King Richard's Grave in Leicester', *Trans. Leics. Arch. Hist. Soc.* LX (1986), 21-4 for the most authoritative up-to-date comment on this.

SELECT BIBLIOGRAPHY

Principal Sources and Chronicles.

York Municipal Records. York City Archives: House Book B2-4. f.169, 169v. See F.Drake, *Eboracum: The History and Antiquities of the City of York* (York, 1736), 120-2; R.Davies, *Extracts from the Municipal Records of the City of York during the Reigns of Edward IV, Edward V, and Richard III* (London, 1843), 214-19; L. Attreed, *York House Books 1461–1490.* 2 Vols. (Stroud: Alan Sutton, 1991)

The Great Chronicle of London. Guildhall Library, London: MSS 3313. See A.H.Thomas and I.D.Thornley (eds.), *The Great Chronicle of London* (London, 1938), 237-8.

The Second Continuation of the Crowland Chronicle. B.L. Cotton MS Otho B xiii. See W. Fulman (ed.), 'Historiae Croylandensis Continuatio', in *Rerum Anglicanum Scriptorum Veterum* I (Oxford, 1684), 573-5; translation in: N. Pronay and J. Cox, *The Crowland Chronicle* Continuations 1459-1486 (London, 1986); H.T. Riley, *Ingulph's Chronicles* (London, 1893), 501-5.

The Letter of Diego de Valera, Castilian councillor, to the King and Queen of Spain. Biblioteca Nacional, Madrid: Codice F.108. See Jose A. de Balenchana (ed.), *Epistolas de otros varios tratados de Mosen Diego de Valera* (Madrid, 1878), 91-6. Translation: E.M. Nokes and G. Wheeler, 'A Spanish Account of the Battle of Bosworth', *The Ricardian* II, no.36 (March 1972), 1-5.

Jean Molinet's Chronicle. Brussels MS 5438, and Paris: Ancuft petit fonds francais, Fr. 24035. See G. Doutrepont and O. Jodogne (eds.), *Chroniques de Jean Molinet* I, 1474-88 (Brussels, 1935), 433-6.

Bosworth Feilde. B.L. Add. MS 27,879 f.434-43. see J. W.Hales and F.J. Furnivall (eds.), *Bishop Percy's Folio Manuscript - Ballads and Romances* III (London, 1868), 233-59.

Harley 542. 'Richard the third, his deathe, by the Lord Stanley, borowyd of Henry Savyll' (The same material as above). B.L. Harley 542 f.31-33v. See J. Nichols, *The History and Antiquities of the County of Leicester* IV (London, 1811), 551-3.

Ladye Bessiye. B.L. Add. MS 27,879 f. 434-43 (Percy folio version, as given in printed edition above); also B.L. Harley 367 f.89-100. See J.O. Halliwell (ed.), 'The Most Pleasant Song of Ladye Bessy', *Percy Society* XX (London, 1847).

The Rose of Englande. B.L. Add. MS 27,879. See J.W. Hales and F.J. Furnivall (eds.), *Bishop Percy's Folio Manuscript - Ballads and Romances* III (London. 1868), 187-194.

Fabyan's Chronicle. Robert Fabyan: *Chronicle* (London, 1516), f.ccxxx.

Polydore Vergil. Polydore Vergil, *Anglica Historia* (Basle, 1534), 554-58. See H. Ellis, (ed.), *Three Books of Polydore Vergil's English History* (Camden Society XXIX, 1844), 221-6 (This is a transcription of the Tudor translation of Polydore Vergil of c.1550, in B.L.MS Royal C, ix.)

Hall's Chronicle. Edward Halle, *The Union of the Two Noble and Illustre Families of Lancastre and Yorke* (London, 1548).

Holinshed's Chronicle. Raphael Holinshed, *The Chronicles of England, Scotland and Ireland....* (London, 1576), 1416-1424.

Some Useful Discussions of the Battle of Bosworth.

M. Bennett, *The Battle of Bosworth* 2nd edition (Stroud: Alan Sutton, 1993).

S.B. Chrimes, *Henry VII* (London: Methuen, 1972).

G.L.Dodds, *Battles in Britain 1066–1746* (London: Arms and Armour Press, 1996)

English Heritage, *The Battlefield of Bosworth Report* (Register of Historic Battlefields, 1995)

P.J. Foss, 'The Battle of Bosworth – Towards a Reassessment', *Midland History* XIII (1988).

P.J.Foss, 'A Significant Document: The Hinckley-Lyre Agreement (1283) and the Site of the Battle of Bosworth', *Hinckley Historian* 22 (Autumn 1988)

J. Gairdner, *History of the Life and Reign of Richard III* (Cambridge: University Press, 1898).

J. Gairdner, 'The Battle of Bosworth', *Archaeologia* LV, i (1896).

A. Goodman, *The Wars of the Roses: Military Activity and English Society 1452-97* (London: Routledge, Kegan Paul, 1981).

R.A. Griffiths and R.S.Thomas, *The Making of the Tudor Dynasty* (Gloucester: Alan Sutton, 1985).

O.D. Harris, ' "... Even here, in Bosworth Field"; A Disputed Site of Battle', *The Ricardian* VII, no.92 (March 1986).

O.D. Harris, 'The Bosworth Commemoration at Dadlington', *The Ricardian* VII, no.90 (September 1985).

R. Holmes, *War Walks II* (London: BBC, 1997)

E.W. Jones, *Bosworth Field... A Welsh Retrospect* (Liverpool and Llandewi Brefi: Modern Welsh Publications Ltd., 1984).

M.J. Phillips, 'The Battle of Bosworth: Further Reflections on the Battlefield Site', *The Ricardian* VII, no.96 (January, 1987).

A.J. Pollard, *Richard III and the Princes in the Tower* (Stroud: Alan Sutton, 1991)

C. Richmond, 'The Battle of Bosworth', *History Today* XXXV (August, 1985)

C. Ross, *The Wars of the Roses* (London: Thames and Hudson, 1976).

C. Ross, *Richard III* (London: Methuen, 1981).

APPENDICES
Appendix I: The Archaeological Problem

Two surprising facts have emerged about the archaeology of the battle of Bosworth. To begin with, most of the known artefacts associated with the battle are not now thought to date from the fifteenth century; and secondly, there has been little systematic archaeological examination of any site within the area of the battlefield.[1] My purpose here is to provide a summary of the present state of knowledge beginning with a list of the artefacts kept in the Leicestershire Museums Collection, most of which were deposited as battle artefacts many years ago, but with no detailed provenance apart from the ubiquitous 'found on Bosworth field'. These are given in chronological order of deposit in the museum collection.

A: The Leicestershire Museums Collection

1   **Halberd head** (2250'1849). $19^1/_4$" by 6". Thought now to be of 17th/18th century date, possibly belonging to a watchman or local sergeant of militia. Possibly the one mentioned in *Catalogue of Mechanics Institute* (1840), 46, no.30.

2   **Dagger hilt with Pommel** (2252'1849). 7" by 4". This has recently been dated by Dr. Sarah Bevan, keeper of Edged Weapons, Royal Armouries, to the last decade of the 15th or first decade of the 16th century. See *London Museums Medieval Catalogue* VII, pp.42, Fig. 10.7.

3   **Cast-iron cannon ball** (97'1891). 2" diam. 'Found just below the surface in Bosworth Field, 1837'. Presented to the museum by Jonathan Smith of Southampton in 1891. This is now thought (by G. Rimer of the Royal Armouries) to be of the Civil War period, though still uncertain.[2]

4   **Silk Material Fragment** (154'1933) 'Supposed to be carried by Richard III at Bosworth Field'. Donated by J.C. Band, Coventry (via Coventry museum). Doubtful but unproven.

5   **Pottery mammiform costrel or water-bottle** (63'1951). Found 'on Bosworth Field'. Late 15th century in date, but provenance vague.

6   **Bronze spurs** (5 I'1958/i). Approx $4^1/_2$" by $2^3/_4$". Found by Canon W.E. Pilling, rector of Market Bosworth, 'tucked away among some old registers' in a safe in Bosworth church vestry in 1958. Now dated to the 17th century. This item probably corresponds with the spurs described in Nichols IV, 557, as 'preserved in the church chest at Bosworth' in 1811.

7   **Sword fragment** (5 I'1958/ii). The same history as no.6. This is now considered to be a funerary weapon made for display over a tomb, and later than 1485.

8   **Spear-head** (319'1958). 15" by 2". Rusted, with two flanges. Deposited by Mr. D. Chaplin of Fields Farm, Sutton Cheney, in 1958. Found on a ledge in an outhouse of the farm. Dated by H. Russell Robinson of the Royal Armouries to the 16th century, and could be a hunting spear.

9   **Silk material fragment 2** (574'1966). $4^1/_3$" by $1^1/_2$". Red painted silk. This has a complicated history. It is said to have been found in 1911 in a bureau at the George and Dragon Inn, Newbold Verdon, after the death of the proprietor's wife, Mrs Hargrave. Examined by D. King of the Victoria and Albert Museum in 1966, it could be of the age ascribed to it. Apart from that, inconclusive. See *Coalville Times* 17 March 1967; P. Tudor-Craig, *Richard III Catalogue* (London, 1973), 72.[3]

B: Antiquarian References

A second area which needs defining is what one may call the antiquarian archaeology, that is, references from the eighteenth or early nineteenth centuries to 'finds' within the area of the battlefield, which have been associated with the battle of Bosworth but which are not now traceable. These are of varying degrees of reliability, for usually anything old and military-looking found within a wide area between Hinckley and Bosworth has tended to be associated with the battle.

The earliest report of finds is probably the most significant: that of William Burton in *The Description of Leicestershire* of 1622. Burton writes that c.1600, at the enclosure of Stoke Golding, a great store of arrow-heads was dug up, some of which were then in his possession (p.47). He further records 'Armour, Weapons and warlike accoutrements frequently found' on the plain between the villages of Shenton, Sutton, Dadlington and Stoke (wording taken from the unpublished 1642 edition, Staffordshire Record Office 649/4/3). Such references suggest that in all likelihood the battlefield had been robbed of any remaining material within 150 years of the battle, very likely during the reclamation of marginal land for enclosure. The material Burton describes does not seem to have survived or to be identifiable among remaining collections.[4]

William Hutton reports several stories about finds in his 1788 book, but he is not a reliable witness. His most significant information may be that of the 'three or four cannon balls, of a smallish size' found in Hewit's garden on Ambion Hill in the mid-eighteenth century. (p.82).[5] Of other finds, he lists two sword blades (no provenance, p.136), a sword and a candle-stick dug out of the sand-pit on Ambion (no date and reported second-hand, p.137), and a sword found in a new gravel-pit at Stoke Golding (no date and reported second-hand, p.137).

Nichols' information is better documented. For example, in his section on Dadlington in *The History and Antiquities of Hinckley* (1782), he writes 'in the field still known by the name of "Crown Hill", whence gravel is sometimes fetched to repair the highways... there have been dug up many human skeletons, which are said to be very common on breaking fresh ground.' (p.100-1). Nichols' list of artefacts in his *History and Antiquities of Leicestershire* IV, ii (1811), 557-8, is as follows:

1   **Processional cross.** $22^1/_2$" by $10^1/_2$". 'Ploughed up about the year 1788, but in what particular part of the field cannot now be properly ascertained'; this according to a letter from a Mr. Sharp of Coventry (where in 1793 the crucifix remained in the possession of Joseph Carter, sexton at St. Michael's). It now belongs to the Society of Antiquaries. Sharp's story of the provenance of the cross persuaded Nichols that it was probably found at Husbands Bosworth, Leicestershire, since from the time of its discovery it had been in the possession of the Fortescue family of Husbands Bosworth Hall. Lady Fortescue gave it to her servant who then left it to the sexton of St. Michael's in 1791. It is doubtful, therefore, that it had any association with the battle of Bosworth. See *Proceedings of the Society of Antiquaries*, 2nd.ser., VIII (1881), 541; P. Tudor-Craig, *Richard III Catalogue* (1973), 77.

2   **Jewel.** Enamelled with a scene of the battle of Bosworth of the time of Henry VIII. This was supposed to have been sold among Charles I's effects (unprovenanced, lost).

3   **Gilt spurs.** From the parish chest at Bosworth, possibly the same as those in Leicestershire Museums Collection (see no. 6).

4   **Brass thumb-ring.** 'Found in the same field'. In Nichols' possession in 1811 (Undated, unprovenanced, lost).

5 **Gold seal-ring.** Enamelled with the figure of a boar and the motto 'S ffrench' or 'S ttianche'. In the Devonshire Collection at Chatsworth. Dated to 1483-5 but unprovenanced. See comments by P. Tudor-Craig, *Richard III Catalogue* (1973), 77.

6 **Amulet or charm.** Noted in a Catalogue of Richard Greene's Museum at Lichfield where it is described as a 'ring of brass found on the field of battle, near Bosworth'. Richard Greene died in 1793, and most of his collection was purchased by a W.A. Yate of Bromesberrow Place, Gloucs. (Undated, unprovenanced, lost).

7 **Crossbow shaft.** From the same museum, although the illustration in Nichols suggests a 17th century date. (Undated, unprovenanced, lost).

8 **Full-hilt sword.** 4' long. Originally in the possession of the Darker family of Barwell, though a Winter Darker was a pre-enclosure land-holder in Sutton Cheney. It was sold to Richard Fowke's Museum at Elmesthorpe before 1811. The illustration in Nichols is clearly of a 17th century cavalier rapier. (Unprovenanced, lost).

9 **Sword.** Fig. 5 in Nichols; also probably of the 17th century, reported to have been at Orton-on-the-Hill.

10 **Sword-hilt.** Fig. 6 in Nichols; reported to have been at Rothley. Now at Newarke Houses Museum, Leicester, and reckoned to be of the 17th century.

11 **Ornate spurs.** Figs. 7a & b in Nichols. Destroyed in the blitz which damaged Liverpool Museum in 1941, together with the records. They appear to be of 17th century date. For comparison, see E. Oakeshott, *European Weapons and Armour* (London, 1980), 166, and plate 11b.

12 **Two spear-heads.** Figs. 8-9 in Nichols. They appear to be of the Bronze Age.

13 **Knife.** 'Found in the Duke of Norfolk's camp'. Appears to be of 17th century date. The 'Duke of Norfolk's camp' was situated adjacent to Sutton brook north of Sutton Cheney, according to the key to Pridden's map in Nichols. Gairdner suggested that he meant Northumberland's camp, but there is no authority for either. Nichols records that the wood here was cleared in 1748, and a hoard of weapons and armaments was unearthed. These items then came into the possession of the Dixies of Bosworth Hall. This is plausible to the extent that at the enclosure of Sutton Cheney the Dixie holding of 40 acres within the open fields of Sutton was consolidated into an allotment adjacent to Sutton brook bordering the Dixie estate, where the meadow was indeed called Wood Meadow. The items seem now to be lost.

14 **Bridle.** Figs. 11a & b in Nichols. 'Found in the field'. Nichols doubted its authenticity, and so must we! Possibly the same reported to be kept in Fowke's Museum at Elmesthorpe: Nichols IV, ii, 605.

C: Further Miscellaneous Recorded Items

1 **Helmet.** 'Found in Bosworth-field, now in the collection of Captain Robson'. Illustrated in F.Grose, *A Treatise on Ancient Armour* (1786), pl.XXX. Appears to be of late 16th century date (Information from Mr. R. Knowles).

2 **Cast-iron cannon-ball.** 'Found upon Amyon-hill, in Bosworth-field... in digging for a post-hole a few years since.' (J. Throsby, *Select Views in Leicestershire* (1789), I, 340). Throsby continues: 'At the same time and place, some pieces of iron and brass resembling coffin handles were discovered, which (Mr. Jee) thinks might be pieces of armour. The ball is 3lb weight, and appears to be cast metal. In Upton lordship, a mile from Amyon hill, was found a ball about a pound weight. Two balls, Mr. Jee informs me, were found upon or near Amyon

Hill, which were some time shewn chained together, at a house in Sutton Cheynell.'
Throsby says the cannon-ball was at Mr. Jee's of Peckleton Hall; it is still there, and is
approximately $2^3/_4$" diameter and 9" circumference.

3 **Halberd.** 'Found in the roof of an old house at Stapleton, near to Bosworth Field, which is
supposed to have been preserved by the ancient family of Dawes of that place'. 9' long,
with oak shaft and banded iron-work, studded with brass nails and with open-work wings.
See *The Gentleman's Magazine* pt.1 (1815), 210. Illustrated in Nichols I, ii, 249, fig.3. It
appears to be of 17th century date: see for comparison E. Oakeshott, *European Weapons
and Armour* (1980), 46, fig. J.

4 **Armour and weapons.** 'Constantly found in ploughing parts of [Col. Wollaston's estate at
Shenton]. Many relics of this important battle are preserved in the hall at Shenton.' W.
Gardiner, *Music and Friends* II (London, 1838), 591-2. (Items donated to Leics. museums by
Mr. H.C. Wollaston before 1951 are not earlier than the 17th century.)

5 **Three items** were exhibited at a Leicestershire Archaeological Society meeting in 1861. 'A
sword from Bosworth field' (27 May 1861); 'a hunting knife (and fork) and cannon ball' -
thought to be of the Civil War if anything (25 November 1861); and a '1670' dated sword
found in a drain near Bosworth. (*Transactions of the Leicestershire Archaeological Society* II
(1861), 40, 87, 92.)

6 **Cannon balls.** A.H. Burne in *The Battlefields of Britain* (London, 1950), 151, reported a stone
cannon ball found c.1935, 150 yards due east of King Richard's Well, by Mr. Bradley of
Ambion Hill Farm; and in c.1946, a stone cannon ball about 4" diameter, found in the field
between Glebe farm and the summit of Ambion Hill.

D: References to Burials

1 **Rough Meadow 'burial'.** In about 1812 'when the late Mr. Morris of Sutton Fields was
making a drain some eight feet deep in what he called "Rough meadow", he found a large
deposit of human and horse bones, covered over with oak boughs before the earth was
cast over them. With these was found the head of a halbert, and near the thigh bone of
one of the skeletons a quantity of common nuts....' (*Transactions of the Leicestershire
Archaeological Society* II (1870), 145 n.) The note goes on to suggest that the evidence of
the nuts makes it unlikely the burial was associated with the battle of Bosworth, but more
likely with the Civil War skirmish of 1 July 1644. D.T. Williams in *The Ricardian* (September
1985), p. 93, disagrees and goes on to identify Rough Meadow as belonging to Ambion
Hill Farm, and therefore to be upon Ambion Hill. However, this is unlikely, particularly since
the Morris family farmed Sutton Fields Farm in 1812. Rough Meadow is more likely to be
one of the closes adjacent to Sutton brook.

2 **Dadlington skeletons (recorded).** 'A grave being prepared for the interment of Mr John
Geary [to the right of the entrance gate] ... about two feet below the ground surface [were
found] twenty skulls. There is no doubt that these are the relics of those who were engaged
and fell in that memorable battle'. (*Hinckley Parish Magazine, Village Advertiser and Local
Church Intelligencer* (1868), 105). 'Skeletons and broken fragments of rusty armour still
frequently obstruct the peasant's plough' (*Leicester Chronicle,* 2 September 1882, p.6).
'Vestiges of the conflict in the shape of rusty arms and co. are still discoverable in the
immediate neighbourhood of the church' (*Leicester Journal* 18 July 1890, p.8). 'While digging
a trench 4' deep for a sewer across land at the back of Rose Cottage... Mr. John Stokes...
found a human skeleton... about 40 yards away from the churchyard' (*Leicester Advertiser*

24 January 1964). 'Bones – numerous – were found at the n. east end of Dadlington ch.y.' (Notebook, c.1880-90, of Thomas Harrold of Hinckley. Information from Mr. David Knight)
3 **Stoke Lodge burial.** About 1900 a 'man in armour' was unearthed 2' below ground on the land of R.H. Roberton, Stoke Lodge, Stoke Golding. It was reported to have 'crumbled to dust' (W.T. Hall., *A Collection for a History of Stoke Golding* (the author, 1928), 80). This may have occurred during the construction of a wind-pump in the field adjacent to the present St. Martin's Convent, at SP 411 972.

E: Unrecorded Items and 'Burials'

1 **Stoke Lodge Skeleton.** Armoured man (?) unearthed c.1936 under peat in a spinney at SP 412 972: 'disintegrated on exposure'. (Information from Mr. R. Gosling of Manor Farm, Dadlington).
2 **Dadlington 'burials'.** Layers of compacted skeletons unearthed in Dadlington churchyard by the former sexton, Jack Simpson, when digging a grave in c.1950. This was on the right of the church path just inside the gate and was remarkable enough to draw a crowd (Information from Mr. R. Gosling, Manor Farm, Dadlington, whose father witnessed this and the above).
3 **Two 'cannon balls'** found on Ambion Hill by Mr. D. Chaplin of Fields Farm, Sutton Cheney, in c.1964 and 1970 (roughly at SK 400 003). One of these, $2^{1}/_{2}$" diameter, seems to be a flint nodule; the other, $3^{1}/_{2}$" diameter, seems to be of a kind of marble. They remain undocumented.

Notes

1. Little work has been done in Britain on the archaeology of battlefields. Fieldwalking and detector surveys of sample 100m. squares across Ambion Hill have so far (1997) been without result (pers. comm. Peter Liddle). The excavation of a mass grave pit at Towton in 1996 constitutes the only such archaeological work done on a medieval battle site in Britain. It identified 43 individuals, with trauma injuries mainly to the skull, thrown into a shallow pit. See A. Burgess, 'Towton Hall, Towton, North Yorkshire – Archaeological Excavation', Archaeological Services WYAS Report 494 (1997). (My thanks to Paul Wheelhouse, Wakefield.)

2. There are many reported finds of cannon balls associated with the battle of Bosworth, from Hutton (1788) onwards, but very little hard evidence as to their authenticity, due to both lack of systematic investigation and to paucity of knowledge in this area. Apparently, the earliest surviving references to cast-iron balls used in warfare are from the 1490s, though there are authoritative mentions of artillery being used at Bosworth. Once the cast-iron gunshot came into wide usage, there was little change in type up to the early nineteenth century. It would therefore be difficult to distinguish sixteenth century and Napoleonic gun stones. There has also been little work done on stone cannon balls. A quantity of early sixteenth century stone balls was recovered from the Mary Rose, which are of course datable, and an anti-personnel device was also found which made use of flint nodules as shrapnel. See M. Rule, *The Mary Rose* (Leicester 1983). (pers. comm. Ruth R. Brown, Royal Armouries).

3. Items 1, 2, 3, 4, 6 and 8 are also described by Pamela Tudor-Craig in her *Richard III Catalogue* of 1973, pp.72-3.

4. Battlefields were generally cleared after a battle, and then scavenged shortly afterwards. Most of such objects would have had a value for the remaining soldiers and to local inhabitants. In general, English battle sites are poor sources of archaeological weaponry (pers. comm. Thom. Richardson, Royal Armouries). In the case of Bosworth high acidity and oxidation properties in this type of soil will rust metal and dissolve bone carbonate quickly (pers. comm. Alan Cook).

5. Hewit inhabited the former Glebe Farm on the Sutton-Shenton parish boundary on the west side of Ambion Hill. In Hutton's time, he was described as 'upward of four-score' years old. Hewits Closes, bordering the Shenton to Dadlington road near Bradfields's Bridge (across the canal) are marked on the Shenton tithe map of 1849.

Appendix II: The Hinckley-Lyre Agreement (1283)

Hinckley church was given to the Abbey of Lyre, Normandy, probably by Robert le Bossu, first Earl of Leicester, in c.1130. Lyre established a small alien cell, Hinckley priory, adjacent to the church, in the reign of Henry II (after 1154), and the dispute that arose in 1283 involved the allocation of tithes in the chapelries of Stoke, Dadlington, Wykin and the Hyde. Below is the text of the Hinckley-Lyre Agreement of 1283, together with an eighteenth century translation.

The translation first appeared in the *Hinckley Church and Parish Magazine* of June 1911 n.s.246, where the provenance is given as Mr. E.H. Gilbert of Coventry Road, Hinckley.[1] Mr. Gilbert purchased four documents from a bookseller in London some time prior to 1911, three in Latin and the fourth the translation provided. The date on the translation – 1742 – suggests that it was made at the time of a Chancery suit brought by the historian, Thomas Carte, in order to recover tithes in Hyde chapelry which had been owing for fifteen years to his late brother, John Carte, vicar of Hinckley from 1720 to 1735. Carte's suit is reported in *Atkyns's Cases* ('Carte versus Ball et al. 13 May 1747').[2] Here it is shown that, although the copy of the document was presented as proof that tithes were originally paid by virtue of this agreement, the document was refused to be admitted as evidence since it did not appear to come 'out of the charter-house of the abbot'. The certification and signature of the then abbot, Prince Louis-Constantine de Rohan-Guéméne, Cardinal-Bishop of Strasbourg (1734- 1779), were not sufficient.

It would seem then that Carte's copies came into Mr. Gilbert's hands in c.1911, but their whereabouts are now unknown. However, a transcription of the Latin text of the 1742 copy seems to have been made before 1911 by Abbé Charles Guéry, the historian of Lyre Abbey. He included it in a notebook cartulary he made of the Abbey charters during his researches at the turn of the century, and he placed beneath his copy the English subscription 'Attested at Lyre, Nov. 14, 1742, by Frat. Jos. Mullot. Calleriargarde des Chartes'.[3]

The accuracy of this copy is confirmed by the details of the Agreement and the rendition of the early forms of the names of Hinckley's chapelries – together with the 'Redemor' itself – which would have been unfamiliar to an eighteenth century French monk. It is also confirmed by the fact that an *Inventory* of the charters of Lyre compiled in 1738-9 on the authority of Prince Louis-Constantine, and under the direction of his proxy Monsignor de Bence, includes a summary of the original charter (now lost) as follows:

> *Transaction entre l'abbaye de Lyre et le vicaire perpétuel de l'église de Hinkelay au sujet de la pension qui luy ajugée sur les dixmes et sur les révénus de lad. eglise pour sa subsistence et celle des prêtres qui desserviront, aux frais dud. vicaire, lad. église et les chapelles en dépendantes.*[4]

Notes

1. The document is discussed in H.J.Francis, *A History of Hinckley* (Hinckley 1930), 33. There is also a (faulty) transcription in W.T.Hall, *A Collection for a History of Stoke Golding* (the author, 1928), 3.

2. See J.Nichols, *History and Antiquities of Hinckley* (London, 1782), 181-2. For a fuller discussion of the survival of this charter see P.J.Foss, 'A Significant Document; The Hinckley Lyre Agreement (1283) and the Site of the Battle of Bosworth', *The Hinckley Historian* 22 (Autumn, 1988)

3. Ref: Archives départementales, Évreux, Eure, France 3F 393/3, pp.493-5. The transcription follows a list of the priors of Hinckley from a manuscript of Bishop Kennett in the British Museum.

4. Archives départementales, Évreux, Eure, France H 590. Volume IV of the *Inventory,* Chapter 97, no. 87.

Accord ou transaction entre le Vicaire perpétuel de Hinckley et l'Abbé et Religieux de l'Abbaie de Lyre

Anno Domini M. CC. octogesimo tertio die jovis, quarto Idus Junii, cum inter nos Magistrum Gilbertum de Burstall perpetuum vicarium, Ecclesie de Hinckelay actorem ex parte una et nos Religiosos viros Abbatum et Conventum de Lyre praedictam ecclesiam in proprios usus habentes et Priorem et monachos de Hinckelay dictis Abbati et conventii pleno jure subjectos et eandem Ecclesiam nomine dictorum Abbatis et Conventiis possidentes Reos ex allera; super proventibus et obventionibus dicte Ecclesie quibus vicarius ejusdem congrue posset sustentari et honera vicarie sue incumbentia supportare, coram Venerabili patre Domino Olivero Lincolniensis Episcopo, non ex delegatione Apostolica causa seii questio verteretur, lis inter nos sopita est concordita in hunc modum videlicet quod ego prefatus Gilbertus toto tempore quo dictam tenuero vicariam et ibidem ut vicarius ministavero sequerer taxationem dicto vicario factam per bone memorie Henricum quondam Lincolniensem Episcopum, praeter meipsum, duos sustentabo presbiteros, unum continue ministrantem in capella de Stokes et alium omni septimana per tres dies divina celebrantem in capella de Dadelington et semel in anno scilicet die Sancti Leonardi in capella de Vike, et semel in anno die S.Laurentii in capella de Hyda ministros mihi et dictis presbiteris idoneos solvam synodalia.

Nos vero prefati Religiosi juxta eandem taxationem cedimus et concedimus dicto Magistro Gilberto toto tempore quo dictam vicariam tenuerit et in ea ministraverit totum alteragium ipsius Ecclesie et minutas decimas ipsuis parochie, exceptis decimis lane et agnorum de Villis de Hinckelay, Daddington et Vike et exceptis principalibus legatis sive fuerint animalia sive res alie in Hinckelay, Daddington et Vike et in Stokes, si principale legatum fuerit averium unum et excepta candela die Purificationis beate Marie et quacumque oblatione ejusdem diei de cunctis villis parochie de Hinckelay praeterquam de Stokes ubi predictus Gilbertus quaslibet oblationes percipiet dicta die; et ubi dictus Gilbertus juxta memoratam taxationem debuit annuatim percipere a Priore de Hinckelay quinque quarteria frumenti et quinque siliginis concedimus ei in commutationem pro dictis quarteriis omnes decimas majores et minores (preter decimam feni) et omnes proventus alios de Capella de Hyda et de quatuor parochionis nostris manentibus in villa de Barewel et concedimus ei sex Rodas prati in Redemor in campis de Daddington quos dictus Gilbertus solvabit suis sumptibus et levabit. Et insuper concedimus ei unam marcam annui redditus quam parochiani capelle de Daddelingtona solvunt annuatim pro campana tribus diebus per hedomadam habenda in eadem capella. Et concedimus insuper eidem Gilberto duo quarteria frumenti annuatim percipienda de grangia nostra apud Hinckelay in festo Sancti Michaelii et totum alteragium capella de Stokes excepto principali vivo et unum messagium in villa de Stokes in quo presbiter ibidem divina celebrans manere consuevit. Et ego prefatus Gilbertus pro predictus concessione et commutatione omni liti hac occasione renuntians promitto dictis religiosis in verbo sacerdotum et sub religione prestiti ipsis fidelitatis sacramenti tenere ipsis fuimiem et perpetuam pacem supra premissis et onera dicte vicarie incumbentia supportare nec non et extraordinaria pro mea portione; ita tamen quod dicti Religiosi Episcopalia et Archidiaconalia praeter synodalia onera sustineant; conventum est etiam quod ego praefatus Gilbertus habeam singulis annis herbagium cimeterii de Hinckelay ex parte ipsius Ecclesie boreali et quod nos prefati Prior et monachi reliquam partem herbagii dicte cimeterii integre et perfecte habeamus et in praemissorum concordita a praedictis partibus actorum et concessorum testimonium presens scriptum per incisionem duplicatum, appositus parti penes dictum Gilbertum remanenti sigillo communi nostro dictorum prioris et monachorum et parti penes nos ipsos remanenti sigillo mei Gilberti Vacarii ante dicti, apud Hinckelay anno et die predictis.

Attested at Lyre Nov. 14, 1742, by Frat. Jos. Mullot Calleriargarde des Chartes.

Translation: from The Hinckley Church and Parish Magazine n.s. 246 (June 1911).

A.D. 1283 on Thursday June 10th, whereas a Cause or dispute hath been carrying on between us Master Gilbert De Burstall, perpetual Vicar of the Church of Hinckley, Complainant, of the one part, and us, the Religious Men the Abbot and Convent of Lyra, enjoying the said Church for our own uses, and the Prior and Monks of Hinckley who are entirely subject to the said Abbot and Convent, Defendents on the other, about the profits and Obventions of the said Church, that may serve for a competent maintenance of the said Vicar and enable him to support the burthen incumbent on his Vicarage, before the venerable Father in God Oliver, Bishop of Lincoln, not acting in virtue of any Delegation from the See of Rome, the Suit between us hath been amicably accommodated in this manner. viz - That I the aforesaid Gilbert shall during all the time that I shall hold the said Vicarage and shall officiate there as Vicar follow the taxation of the said Vicarage made by Henry of pious memory, formerly Bishop of Lincoln, and I will besides myself maintain two presbyters, one officiating constantly in the Chapel of Stoke, and the other saying Divine service three days in every week in the Chapel of Dadlington, and once a year, viz., on St. Leonard's Day in the Chappel of Wyken, and once a year on St. Lawrence's Day in the Chapel of Hyde, and also fit Ministers for me and the said presbyters, and will pay Synodals - And we the aforesaid Religious do according to the said Taxation Yield and Grant to the said Master Gilbert during all the time he shall hold the said Vicarage and officiate therein All the Altarage of the said Church and the Small Tythes of the said parish, except the Tythes of Wool and Lamb of the Towns of Hinckley, Dadlington and Wyken, and except the Mortuaries whether Beasts or other things in Hinckley, Dadlington and Wyken, and in Stoke if the Mortuary be one Beast for the plough, and except a Candle on Candlemas Day, and all Oblations on the said Day in all the Towns of the Parish of Hinckley except Stoke where the said Gilbert shall receive all the Oblations on the said Day. And whereas the said Gilbert ought according to the said Taxation to receive annually from the prior of Hinckley 5 quarters of wheat and 5 of the finest wheat flour, we grant him by way of exchange for the said quarters all the great and small Tythes (except Tythe Hay) and all other profits of the Chapel of Hyde and of our four parishioners residing in the Town of Barewell and we grant him 6 roods of Meadow in Redemore in the Fields of Dadelinton which the said Gilbert shall mow and carry away at his own charge, and we likewise grant him one Mark of yearly rent which the parishioners of the chapel of Dadelinton pay yearly for having a Bell three days a week in the said chapel. And we further grant to the said Gilbert 2 quarters of wheat to be received annually from our grange at Hinckley on Michaelmas Day and all the Altarage of the Chapel of Stoke (except the Mortuary, if it be an animal) and one Messuage in the Town of Stoke, in which the priest there officiating is used to dwell. And I the said Gilbert in consequence of the said Grant and Exchange, renouncing all litigation on this occasion, do promise the said Religious in the word of a priest, and under the Obligation of the Oath of Fidelity which I have taken to them, to keep the peace forever with them in respect of the premises, and will bear all the burthens incumbent on the said Vicarage as also such Extraordinaries as fall to my share; provided still that the said Religious discharge all the Dues to the Bishop and Archdeacon except Synodales. It is agreed likewise that the said Gilbert shall have every year the Herbage of the Church Yard at Hinckley on the north side of the said Church, and that we the said prior and Monks shall have fully and entirely the rest of the Herbage of the said Church Yard. And in Testimony of the premises agreed to be done and granted by the aforesaid parties we have put our Seals to an indented Duplicate of the present Writing, the Common Seal of us the said prior and monks being put to the part which is to be kept by the said Gilbert, and the Seal of me Gilbert the Vicar aforesaid being put to the part which remains with us at Hinckley, the day and year above mentioned.

INDEX